FRANKEN

Lovely
FRANCONIA

FRAN
Lovely
FRANCONIA

Imprint:
Second revised Edition: 2007
©Elmar Hahn Verlag, Raiffeisenstrasse 2, 97209 Veitshöchheim – www.elmar-hahn-verlag.de
No part of this publication may be reproduced in any form or by any means, electronic, digital
or otherwise without the written approval of the publishing house.

Idea and Concept: Elmar Hahn, Klaus Schinagl
Photography: Elmar Hahn
except for:
Herbert Liedel (cover, inside front cover, back cover, pages: 17, 116/117, 120/121, 124/125, 132, 141 oben, 150 to 153, 155 below, 158 to 161, 164, 165, 174 to 177, 180 to 193, 198 to 201, 204 to 209, 216, 218 to 224, 226, 288, 299 above);
Thomas Peter Widmann (pages: 9, 14, 118/119, 210/211, 214/215, 224/225, 226 above, 234/235, 236/237, 239, 241, 243, 244 above and below, 246/247, 248 above, 251 to 253, 256 to 261, 266 to 271, 274/275, 276 to 277, 278/279, 280, 281 to 285, 290 to 291, 295, 297, 298, 299 below, 300 to 304);
Rainhard Feldrapp (pages: 236, 238, 240/241, 245, 248 below, 272/273, 274, 278, 292 to 294);
Anton Kaiser (pages: 30/31, 32/33); Hans Raab (pages: 136, 156); Jürgen Wackenhut (pages: 147, 155 above, 173); German Rail Museum, Nuremberg (pages: 16/17); Foto Engel (pages: 262/263, 264/265); Berndt Fischer (pages: 280); Wolfgang Grötsch (pages: 121, 128 to 131, 133 to 135); Helmut Gruber (pages: 144/145); Cornelia Haas (pages: 55); Jürgen Holzhausen (pages: 24/25, 26/27); Thomas Huth (pages: 13); Staatliche Kurverwaltung Bad Kissingen (pages: 37); Landesbibliothek Coburg (inside back cover); Guido Mehl (pages: 166); Wolfgang Pusch (pages: 22/23); Süßmann (pages: 300); Josef Stöhr (pages: 148/149); Toni Schneider (pages: 170 above); Michael Vogel (pages: 167, 196/197)

Text: Thomas Huth
English Interpretation: Dr. Terence Zuber, New Martinsville, WV
Layout: Design by Klaus Schinagl, Veitshöchheim
Production: Druckerei Theiss GmbH, St. Stefan im Lavanttal – www.theiss.at

ISBN 978-3-928645-31-7

Following pages: The Main River waterway near the town of Volkach.

IKEN

Photography: Elmar Hahn,
            Herbert Liedel,
            Thomas Peter Widmann
            and others
      Text: Thomas Huth
   English: Terence Zuber
   Layout: Klaus Schinagl

elmar
hahn
verlag

The Franconian Panorama

Franconia - does it really exist? There's no state called Franconia on a German map. Only the close observer will notice that in the northern part of Bavaria, geographical terms such as Franconian Forest, Franconian Switzerland and Franconian Plateau appear. Not to alleviate the matter in any way is the additional problem of Franconia being divided into three individual regions known as Upper, Middle and Lower Franconia. Thus Franconia does exist and it is waiting to be explored. This region doesn't force itself upon the traveler; in fact, it remains a little aloof. Touristing in Franconia is well worth the effort. The description a 19th century German poet, Karl Immermann, gave of Franconia, is still appropriate today. Immermann compared Franconia to a magical armoire whose drawers upon opening were continually filled with new surprises.

These drawers are brimming over with history. Franconia was the connecting link between north and south Germany and it served as a transit land between east and west. Approaching from northern Germany, the traveler gets his first taste of the sunny south in the Main-Franconian region. The Bavarians and Austrians, on the other hand, consider Franconia as a more northerly region due to its fair amount of Protestantism. The sensuous jubilance of the Baroque style is as much at home here as the old half-timbered towns reminiscent of those along the Rhine. Franconia actually offers the traveler a look at Germany in miniature. This is due in great part to the centuries of struggles for power among the clerics, the counts and the margraves in this region.

The photographers, Elmar Hahn, Thomas Widmann and Herbert Liedel have combined their talents and filled this „Franconian magical armoire" with a carefully-selected array of color photographs that both inspire and delight the traveler while documenting the variety of Franconian culture and heritage in the midst of an unusually scenic countryside. The text, based on the old saying „you only see what you know", attempts to give some background information and insight into the pictures to help the traveler along the way. The graphic artist, Klaus Schinagl, has successfully created a layout design that makes this travel guide a truly magical „Franconian Experience". My hope is that this pleasant guide will enable the traveler to more readily enjoy the attractions and sights of lovely Franconia!

Table of Contents

Franconia in Bavaria

"It would be a shame if the word Franconia were to die out and be replaced by the term Bavaria!" These were the sentiments of Karl Julius Weber, a German satirist, in 1826. His concern was not without cause because in Weber's time, the regions now known as Lower, Middle and Upper Franconia were then called Lower Main, Upper Main and Rezat Districts. Due to secularization and the new Bavarian rulers, the name Franconia was in danger of disappearing from the consciousness of the Franconians and the map of Germany. It wasn't until the administrative reform in 1837 that the individual Bavarian districts were guaranteed their historically-significant names. The Franconians on the Main, Regnitz and Altmühl rivers were officially permitted to remain Franconian although one small hitch was attached: these inhabitants were first and foremost Bavarian citizens and then Franconians.

Jokes have been making the rounds ever since as to the relationship between the real Bavarians and the new Franconians. The saying goes that Franconia is a hard nut to crack in the mouth of the Bavarian lion. "Old" Bavarians have always been afraid that their homeland would be ruled solely by Franconians. Other cliches are even more direct such as "We must thank God for everything He has given us, even Lower Franconians". Proof that Franconians can hold their own is found in the remark made by a former Franconian undersecretary when he compared the traditionally Bavarian, plump weisswurst to the slender bratwurst eaten throughout Franconia: "The Bavarians have the mountains, the Franconians the horizon!"

Franconian and Free

Enough on "bantering one's rival". It is interesting to look a bit more closely as to why Franconians are so proud of their identity which is so ingrained in their history. Their name is derived from the Germanic tribe of the Franks, who were known in history as the leading tribe in the Empire of the Merovingians and Carolingians. Germany's neighbor to the west, France, derives its name from the peoples and the empire of the Franks as well. The Franks were at home along the lower Rhine. After the fall of the Roman Empire, they were able to expand their power to the south and southeast. After defeating their rivals, the Alemanni, and the Thuringians, in the 5th and 6th centuries, there was nothing to stop the Franks from moving into the Main River region. Alemanni and Thuringians as well as Celts and Slavs were also at home in this region but the Franks were able to take over and expand their influence. The region became Frankish. True to their name,

which roughly translates into "free man", they weren't subordinate to anyone. "Franconian and free", a motto of the Franks, is as fitting today as in the days of the Empire.

Franconia shared the fate of the Frankish Empire and later, the Holy Roman Empire of the German Nation. The duchy in Franconia was especially important to the Empire during the Middle Ages. However, Ottonian and Salian Franconia included large portions of the state of Hesse and Rhineland-Palatinate and was therefore considerably larger than Franconia is today.

Three Irish Apostles Bring Christianity to Franconia

Christianity arrived relatively early in Franconia. The new Frankish rulers brought it with them and numerous waves of missionaries spread Christianity throughout the region. In 742, Boniface, an Anglo-Saxon bishop, was able to found bishoprics in Würzburg and Eichstätt. A good half century early, three missionaries from the British Isles had already caused some commotion in Würzburg when the residing Frankish-Thuringian ducal family converted to Christianity. Kilian, Kolonat and Totnan were the three Irish missionaries who were found decapitated in the year 689. They were soon canonized and Main-Franconia had its very own saints. The Kiliani Celebration each July in Würzburg is still one of the largest folk festivals in Franconia. The church took on a dominant role early on in Franconia. After the ducal family died out, the bishop of Würzburg took advantage of this power vacuum to increase his personal position. The bishop of Eichstätt as well was able to set up a secular state over the course of the Middle Ages. With the founding of the bishopric in Bamberg by Emperor Heinrich II and his wife, Kunigunde, in the year 1007, spiritual trinity in Franconia was complete.

Above: Emperor Heinrich II and his wife, Kunigunde, holding the Bamberg Cathedral as a symbol of their founding of this bishopric.

Left: Kilian's banner from 1266 was the war banner of the bishop of Würzburg.

9

Minnesingers and Free Imperial City Air

Cities began to flourish in Franconia, as elsewhere, during the reign of the Hohenstaufen in the 12th and 13th centuries. It was the church versus the nobility vying for control. Some Franconian cities such as Rothenburg, Schweinfurt, Windsheim, Weissenburg, Dinkelsbühl and Nuremberg were able to win their imperial freedom. These cities freed themselves from their rulers and became self-governing city-republics. Other aspiring cities like Würzburg and Bamberg fought diligently albeit unsuccessfully and not always entirely fairly to free themselves from their spiritual rulers. In addition to the church and the cities, the nobility as well was not shy about taking advantage of the failing influence of the imperial central power. A noble family, the Zollern, from the Swabian Alb achieved the most successful career move. The family used its position as burgraves in the Kaiserburg in Nuremberg to acquire their own territory. The margraves of Ansbach and of Bayreuth created the two largest secular duchies in Franconia from the burgraves in Nuremberg. Missing from this Franconian mosaic are the less significant pieces such as the counts of Wertheim, Rieneck, Hohenlohe, Henneberg, Castell and Pappenheim. These counts were the Franconian imperial knights, and the Knights of the Teutonic Order whose administrative territory in Franconia was considered to be one of the wealthiest in the Order.

The more parceled-off the map of Franconia became, the broader its cultural and artistic diversity spread. Noble families of greater and lesser importance made use of the arts to enhance their growing significance. The first major cultural period is the age of the minnesingers. Franconia was extremely fortunate to have such a high density of poets like Wolfram, the author of Parsifal, who came from the Middle Franconian town of Eschenbach; Otto von Bodenlauben sang from the Franconian Saale River and the German language's most well-known minnesinger, Walther von der Vogelweide, spent his last days in the Main-Franconian region. The multitude of finely-furnished and technically-improved fortresses that were built in the heydays of fortress construction around 1200 offered the ideal setting for these itinerant poets. Henneburg Fortress above Stadtprozelten and Salzburg Fortress near Bad Neustadt still provide a glimpse of the splendor of those days at

court. The best proof of the elegance of the period, however, is the Cathedral in Bamberg which still houses many a sculptural treasure despite having survived some rather rough and unpleasant times. The statue of the Bamberg Knight, who incorporates all the ideals of a knightly life, adorns the inside of the Cathedral.

Dürer, Riemenschneider and the End of the Middle Ages

One city alone, the city of Nuremberg, became the center of culture in Franconia in the late Middle Ages. The free imperial city, that was hardly worthy of notice as late as the 11th century, attracted innumerable craftsmen and was a hub of commerce of European significance into the beginning of the 16th century. The burghers were comfortable with aristocratic life and the way of the clergy since these were the well-heeled customers who could afford the luxury goods and precision instruments the city produced. Well-versed in such matters, the leading families soon turned

to the arts. Around 1500 Nuremberg was not only Franconia's richest city, it was one of the major cultural centers in Germany boasting of artists such as Albrecht Dürer, Veit Stoß and Adam Krafft. A glance at the biographies of the artists of this period reveals how mobile mankind was in the late Middle Ages and how dynamic city development was. Many of Nuremberg's famous burghers came from elsewhere: the Dürer family had immigrated from Hungary a generation earlier and Veit Stoß came from a region along the Neckar River. The medieval city's success in attracting so much talent was due in great part to the fact that it permitted those not privileged by birth to climb the social ladder of acceptance.

It wasn't solely in Nuremberg that newcomers were able to achieve such success. Tilman Riemenschneider in Würzburg was a similar story. Many might want to see this woodcarver who resided in the Franziskanergasse as a typical Franconian. He was, in fact, a self-made man from the Thuringian town of Eichsfeld and remains unequaled in the art of woodcarving. Riemenschneider alone was able to express the gentle contemplation of the Main-Franconian character so completely in his exquisite linden wood figures.

The years before and after 1500 were of extreme importance to the Franconians. Vast parts of the region were flourishing economically and culturally. Lucas Cranach and Matthias Grünewald are two further Franconian artists whose names cannot be forgotten even though their fame was achieved outside of Franconia.

The year 1500 needs to be considered in its historical context as well to help us understand the makeup of the Franconians. In an attempt to reorganize the

Left: In his World Chronicle in 1492, Hartman Schedel portrayed Nuremberg as an economic center of European significance.

Above: Tilman Riemenschneider portrayed himself in the "The Mourning of Christ" in the Maidbronn altar (before 1525).

Holy Roman Empire of the German Nation, Emperor Maximilian had the empire divided into imperial districts. Franconia, known as Frankonia Orientalis, became one of the smallest. The area was comparable to the three current Franconian administrative districts with the exception of the western portion. The name Franconia became fixed in the minds of the region's inhabitants whereas the connection entirely disappeared in the lower and middle Rhine regions, the original home of the Germanic tribe of the Franks. This area became a part of the lower, upper or electorate Rhine region and the word Franconia vanished from the language.

Nowadays, no one in Cologne, Koblenz or Frankfurt has any particular affinity for the word Franconian. Just the opposite is true for Bamberg, Ansbach and Schweinfurt where the establishment of an imperial district in medieval times remains a part of the Franconian heritage.

The Peasants' War and the Reformation brought about vast changes in the lifestyle and social structure of the Middle Ages. Whereas the Peasants' War questioned the whole class system, the Refor-

mation caused an irrevocable split in western and central European views on Christianity. Franconia was also the scene of these developments. In Würzburg, peasants' attempts to besiege the Marienberg and demand equal rights ended in a bloodbath when troops of the nobility and the prince-bishop opened defensive fire. Nuremberg adopted the Reformation in 1524/25 and set an example for other imperial cities in Franconia. Many nobleman followed this example and in the end, only the prince-bishops in Würzburg, Bamberg and Eichstätt as well as the Knights of the Teutonic Order clung to the old church beliefs. A territorial as well as a spiritual division affected life in Franconia and once again, Franconia sampled German conditions on a smaller scale.

The Thirty Years' War Takes a Heavy Toll in Franconia

Franconia, the heartland of the empire, did not go unscathed during the Thirty Years' War either. The theater of war began a good distance from Franconia but the Swedish attacks in the 1630s brought death and destruction to this region as well. The front lines cut straight through a region divided by confession and the continual comings and goings of friend and foe played havoc among the inhabitants. Franconia lost up to one-third of its population either as a direct result of fighting or, as was more often the case, through epidemics that came in waves with the troops. The memory of the horrors of this war are so ingrained in many places that the story is retold year after year in historical plays like the Meistertrunk in Rothenburg or the Children's Festival in Dinkelsbühl. Reconstruc-

Above: Albrecht Dürer's as he saw himself: his inquisitive eyes and fine hands are his trademarks.

Right: The Schönborn family portrayed in the High Altar of the village church in Gaibach: their Baroque faces and attire reveal their influence on the Catholics in Franconia.

tion began after the war ended in 1648. The inhabitants of Nuremberg celebrated by serving a "peace supper" most likely in the hopes of being able to return to grander days. There was one permanent loss: the imperial cities were unable to recover, their territories were far too small in order to compete against the modern principalities with their greater economic influence. Even Nuremberg, once an affluent economic giant had been reduced to a shadow of its former self and at the end of the 18th century asked to be admitted to the Prussian state.

The Baroque Conquers Franconia

While the former imperial cities were stagnating, the palatial cities were flourishing. The refreshing new Baroque style, often imported from Italy, turned medieval towns into modern palatial ones. Würzburg, Bamberg, Bayreuth and Ansbach underwent cosmetic surgery, usually leaving that below the surface unchanged. In the best case scenario, world class architecture was the result as was the case with the prince-bishop's Residence in Würzburg. The Schönborn dynasty that produced more bishops and prince-bishops that probably any other family line, carried out an ambitious project which, thanks to Balthasar Neumann's planning and execution, is one of the outstanding 18th century European palaces. The Schönborns were also active in Bamberg, Pommersfelden, Wiesentheid, Seehof, Werneck and Vierzehnheiligen where the family's sense and perception of the arts makes these places genuine achievements of the Baroque era. The Protestant palatial courts in Bayreuth and Ansbach were equally innovative. Great architecture accomplishments were achieved although purses were not always overflowing, which was especially true in the case of Wilhelmine, the margrave of Bayreuth's wife. Wilhelmine's ethereal creations in the gardens of Sanspareil or her choice of pastels in the New Castle remain unique. Lesser nobility wanted their version of Versailles as well. The princes Löwenstein accomplished such in Kleinheubach on the river Main.

The End of the Old Empire or Franconia Becomes Bavarian

In a nutshell: Franconia managed rather well between the peace treaty in 1648 until secularization in 1803. In Würzburg, the "Schönborn era" had become a household word used to describe the prosperity of the times. An economic wonder made the Baroque and Rococo eras possible. Franconia had had the good fortune to develop a variety of economic tools as no other region had, but it lacked a tradition of autonomy. This became evident when Napoleon marched through and consolidated the splintered sovereignties. As early as the year 1791, the last margrave in Ansbach sold his principality to his Prussian relatives. This left three bishoprics as sovereign rulers in all of Franconia. Due to the collapse of the Holy Roman Empire of the German Nation, they, too, were wiped off the map during the Imperial Diet in Regensburg in 1802/03. Franconia was divided up amongst the victors. Bavaria was the big winner, but Baden, Württemberg and Hesse were able to get their fill on the borders of the former Franconian imperial districts. At the Congress of Vienna, Franconia became a Bavarian province once and for all. Bamberg, Schweinfurt, Nuremberg and Pappenheim no longer enjoyed self-rule. Franconia had to reorient its economic energies. Previous contracts and commissions from the bishoprics or principalities were suddenly non-existent. The new economic center of Munich was far too far away; moreover, there were no previous ties to the Bavarian capital.

The First German Train Connects Nuremberg and Fürth

This involuntary reorientation provided the opportunity to begin anew since being a part of Bavaria did result in several positive changes. Catholics and Protestants were finally officially of equal status and the dissolution of the guilds allowed competition to become keener. In many such instances, this meant a new start for industrialization. Nuremberg, for example, shook itself awake and reminded itself of its former virtues. Within a few decades this sleepy former patrician city turned itself around and became Bavaria's most important industrial city. Obvious proof of the city's forward thinking was validated by the fact that in 1835 Germany's first train ran between two budding industrial hubs, Nuremberg and Fürth.

Industrialization was on the rise elsewhere as was the case in Würzburg where Koenig & Bauer began manufacturing printing press machines for the European market in 1817. Textile and porcelain

Above: Antoine Pesne's portrait of the margrave of Bayreuth's wife, Wilhelmine, a patron of Baroque architecture and design.

Right: A bird's eye view of the fortifications in Würzburg during the Baroque. Johann Baptist Homann designed this copperplate engraving in 1723.

manufacturing found a home in the eastern part of Upper Franconia and Schweinfurt became the ball bearing capital of the world. All these developments seemed to bypass rural Franconia. A Franconian law that decreed farmland was to be divided among all one's sons left farms too tiny to be viable. Whenever possible, young people traded the villages of their youth for the big city or even a stint abroad. The list of emigrants to America is as long as is the list of success stories. Loeb Strauß from Buttenheim near Forchheim emigrated to the US where he eventually began manufacturing Levi Strauss jeans, still the most successful trousers sold worldwide.

It was more than the legal or social conditions that drove young people out of their villages. Nature played its part as well. The damage done to the grapevines by phylloxera plant lice in the 19th century almost completely eradicated Franconian viticulture in the 20th century. In the age of Goethe, Franconian wines covered ten times the surface they do today and Franconia was the number one wine exporter in the empire. Phylloxera plant lice caused a decline that the contemporary wine connoisseur can be grateful for. Nowadays wine can only be grown on climatically-favorable slopes containing specific geological compositions. Indirectly, these plant lice played a role in improving the quality of Franconian wines.

Franconia as a part of Bavaria has had its advantages as well as disadvantages. Franconians have a knack for adapting and they have made the best out of the situation. They have remained true to themselves while adjusting to the new without relinquishing their old ties. The postwar era and the rebuilding of the Old Towns in Würzburg and Nuremberg, which had been reduced to rubble by Allied bombing, created a turbulent, economic upswing that was set off by the

large number of expellees who were forced to start a new life in western Germany. Two or three generations later, these expellees have become dyed-in-the-wool Franconians.

Germany's 17th State?

Franconia has a population of over four million people, around the same number as the state of Rhineland-Palatinate. Many a Franconian patriot has long dreamed of breaking away from Bavaria and becoming a state instead of a mere region. Yet it is probably better to leave things as they are. An old German saying maintains that Franconians are a cantankerous lot and it would not be hard to imagine the quarrels that could develop over who could be considered a Franconian and who not. The biggest problem would be agreeing on a state capital. Should it be Nuremberg, Würzburg or maybe Bamberg? Or should a capital be chosen due to its location in the middle of the new state, perhaps in the somewhat remote Steigerwald Wood? These are actually unnecessary worries since Franconia is part and parcel of the Free State of Bavaria and because of this, Franconians benefit from being both Bavarian and Franconian.

Bytes and Bocksbeutel Bottles

It is important for this region to maintain and preserve its identity and at the same time, be future-oriented and economically viable. It is equally important that Franconians have a say in the state capital in Munich. Franconians can be proud of their unique position and the region's increasing popularity as a vacation spot. Franconian wines sold in belly-shaped Bocksbeutel bottles symbolize the quality and the fine cuisine of the region. Carnival celebrations in the picturesque town of Veitshöchheim attract people from all over the country and offer the opportunity to introduce Germans to the lively quick-wittedness of Franconians living between the Spessart Forest and the Fichtel Hills. From a cultural point of view, Franconia, due to its varied local history and rich heritage, is a real jewel. And the Christkindl Christmas Market in Nuremberg is not only famous in Germany but throughout the world. Equally as notorious and popular are the liter steins of beer and sizzling bratwurst stands as well as the leather shorts and pants men wear in the region. Franconia, in addition to all its traditions and culinary delights,

looks to its future as a significant economic center with high quality educational opportunities. Franconia proudly identifies with both Bocksbeutel bottles and bytes. Large, centuries-old universities in Würzburg and Erlangen provide higher education as well as newer, smaller universities in Bayreuth, Bamberg and Aschaffenburg. Earning a degree or master craftsman's diploma in the region is usually rewarded with finding a position near home. The number of new industries being established here has increased significantly in the last few years. This is a fortunate development since traditional, longstanding industries, be it porcelain or textile manufacturers, are fighting to survive. Several new companies such as GfK in Nuremberg, Adidas, HUK Coburg, S. Oliver and Bionade are examples of the new business look in Franconia. Diversity and flexibility are thriving due to an excellent infrastructure and Franconia's central location not only in Germany but also within the European Union. Scenic beauty spreading from the Rhön Hills to the Franconian Alb Plateau, the Spessart Forest to the Altmühl valley ensures leisure time recreational diversity and a quality of life that is hard to beat. Franconia is optimistic about its future and the new developments in the region. At

the same time, Franconia, be it upper, middle or lower, is taking great care to preserve its cultural heritage and lovely countryside.

Genuine Franconians and newcomers alike enjoy living between the Spessart Forest and the Fichtel Hills. The quality of life and opportunity for leisure time activities alongside the historical cultural cornucopia of the region are reason enough to pause and enjoy. Quoting the 19th century poet, Viktor von Scheffel, who heartily recommended Franconia:

> *I want to travel to*
> *The land of the Franconians*
> *In the heart of the summer!*

But not only in the summertime ...

Left: The "Adler" or Eagle marked the beginning of train travel in Germany. It ran from Nuremberg to Fürth.

Above: Nowhere in Franconia can the celebrations begin until the cut tree stands: this is also the case in Ehrenbürg.

Milestones in the Course of History

Time of Christ's birth	Numerous ring walls and quadrangular earthworks are reminders of the Celtic settlements in Franconia.
1st-3rd century	The area to the left of the Lower Main River and the southerly portion of Middle Franconia are a part of the Holy Roman Empire.
6th century	The region derives its name from the Germanic tribe of the Franks who, having come from the Rhine, settle in the region.
689	Three Irish monks, Kilian, Totnan and Kolonat, die a martyr's death in Würzburg.
704	Würzburg is first officially named in a document.
742/745	Boniface founds the bishoprics of Würzburg and Eichstätt.
793	The first attempt to build a canal, the Fossa Carolina, between the Main and the Danube rivers fails.
1007	Emperor Heinrich II and his wife, Kunigunde, found the bishopric in Bamberg.
1168	Emperor Frederick Barbarossa confers the ducal title on the bishop of Würzburg.
1192	Friedrich von Zollern becomes the burgrave of Nuremberg through his marriage and the Hohenzollern dynasty begins to exert its influence in Franconia.
Circa 1200	Minnesingers thrive in Franconia; around 1230 Walther von der Vogelweide is laid to rest on the grounds of the Neumünster Church.
1219	Emperor Frederick II issues a proclamation to the burghers of Nuremberg granting self-governing status, an important step on the way to imperial freedom.
1356	Emperor Karl IV's Golden Bull is proclaimed in Nuremberg. It establishes the procedures for royal elections and requires the newly-elected king to hold his initial Imperial Diet in Nuremberg.
1402	The first university is established in Franconia in the town of Würzburg. The university has to close its doors a few years later when the rector is murdered.
Circa 1500	Artists and craftsmen such as Riemenschneider, Stoß, Dürer, Krafft, Grünewald and the Vischers, a family of founders, turn Franconia into one of the most highly-artistic cultural landscapes in Germany.
1500	In the course of the reform of the Empire, the East Franconian Imperial Circle is created. This lays the foundation for the preservati-

on of regional identity which is maintained today in lower, middle and upper Franconia.

1525 The peasants rise up against their rulers in many parts of Franconia but especially in the bishopric of Würzburg. The peasants suffer a bloody defeat.

1525 The free imperial city of Nuremberg introduces the Reformation. Most of the other Franconian imperial cities and regions follow suit. Since then, Franconia has been mainly Protestant.

1617-1633 More men and women are condemned to be burned at the stake for witchcraft than anywhere else in Germany.

1618-1648 Franconia suffers from the Thirty Years' War. The principal armies surge back and forth through a country divided along religious lines.

1650-1750 Construction after the Thirty Years' War turns vast portions of Franconia into a land of the Baroque. Patrons of the era are the prince-bishops and the margraves of the Hohenzollern dynasty. Italian masters such as Petrini, Gabrieli and Carlone help lay the foundation stone.

1802-1803 The Empire (Reichsdeputationshauptschluss) secularizes the religious principalities and suppresses the independence of the free imperial cities.

1815 The Congress of Vienna makes Franconia a part of the Kingdom of Bavaria.

1835 The first German train travels from Nuremberg to Fürth.

1846 For the first time, the 173-kilometer long Ludwig-Danube-Main Canal provides a navigational route connecting the Rhine, Main and Danube rivers. A mere twenty years later, this technological masterpiece is no longer profitable.

1852 The German Museum in Nuremberg opens its doors. Nowadays it is renowned as Germany's largest museum for art and culture.

1920 The Coburg portion of the former Saxon-Coburg and Gotha duchy becomes Bavarian and thus a part of Upper Franconia.

1933-1945 Nuremberg is the headquarters of National Socialist party congresses. Allied bombing destroys much of the historical centers of Nuremberg and Würzburg during the final years of the Second World War.

1992 The final section of the Main-Danube Canal, which connects the North Sea to the Black Sea, is officially opened.

1999 The creation of the Plateau of Franconian Lakes is finally completed with the flooding of the large Brombach Lake.

2007 Franconia covers an area of 23,008 km² and has over 4.1 million inhabitants.

UNTERF

Romantic
LOWER FRANCONIA

RANKEN

Barren Summits Predatory Forests and an Ambitious River

The Rhön Region, the Spessart Forest and the Odenwald Wood make up Lower Franconia's medium range wooded hills. The valleys of the Saale, the Sinn and the Main rivers have provided both a cultural and economic lifeline for hundreds of years.

23

Germany's Austere Heartland

Franconia in Bavaria has to share the Rhön region with Hesse and Thuringia and fortunately, the state borders here go unnoticed. It is the land of vast distances, of prominent hilltops, of marshy plateaus and sheep dotting the countryside. The hills were never a barrier; crossing them never presented a real problem. Approaching the region from the north, the traveler has the impression that beyond the hills of the Rhön, southern Germany comes into view. On the other hand, the south German feels that these low hills are a sample of what northern Germany is like. This is truly the middle of Germany. Boniface was well aware of this fact when he founded the eminent monastery in Fulda at the foothills of the Rhön. The monastery was to be the center of religious influence that was to be spread throughout Germany and thus its location was of great significance. Nowadays, over 1200 years later, this same significance is still evident. Franconia's Christian beginnings are connected to the Rhön as well. One of the region's highest

hills, the 928-meter Kreuzberg, is know as Franconia's holy hill. Pious believers still pilgrim each year to the top of the hill where three crosses remind the pilgrim of Franconia's first apostles, Kilian, Kolonat and Totnan. The procession, however, also manages to attract many a beer-lover to the dark brew of the Franciscan monks!

Not the Land of Milk and Honey

The Rhön Hills used to be synonymous with poverty. The soil was barren and there were few natural resources, which often forced the locals to seek work out-side the region. As late as the 19th century the saying still went: "The Rhön provides the most soldiers, clerics and prostitutes". Those who stayed behind often consoled themselves with alcohol. "It's a shame that so many have fallen victim to spirits" are the words of Karl Julius Weber in 1826. Many times the region's inhabitants were so ashamed of their origin that they changed the names of their villages to hide their true locations. Thus

Previous pages: Rhön sheep grazing add a bucolic touch to the scenery.

Below: The tops of the over 900-meter high Rhön Hills appear like islands in a sea of fog.

the town of Bishofsheim became Bishofsheim on the Rhön even though nowadays we would look at the map and see that the town lies nestled among the hills at the foot of the Kreuzberg Hill. The Rhön Region seems to extend to far corners nowadays. The inhabitants of the spa town Bad Kissingen speak of the Rhön, which is an indication of how times change. A region that was once nothing to boast of has become a region famous for its clean air and unspoiled scenic beauty, in other words, the ideal holiday spot in our postmodern society. No longer would one regret being from the Rhön; in fact, it is something to be proud of.

Natural Beauty Combined with Cultural Significance

Geological diversity is as great as the scenery it is a part of. Lone-standing hilltops of volcanic black basalt dominate the landscape alongside the plateaus of the High Rhön. Red variegated sandstone forms the mutual base of the Spessart Forest while the foothills to the south and west are known for their beige and gray shell limestone. Each of these types of rock in conjunction with the varied localized climate create their own fauna and flora, a fact that makes the region one of the most diverse in Germany's hill country. Cotton-grass and sundew grow on the wet moors of the High Rhön. A variety of wild orchid and gentian species, Turk's cap and the pale red and white checkered wild lily, the Fritillaria meleagris, are some of the rare wildflowers found in the Rhön. A stemless species of the silver thistle is a fitting symbol for the region although the grazing sheep alongside it are hardly compatible. When speaking of sheep, we are, of course, speaking of man's continuing

Above: Only the sturdiest of trees can survive in this barren, windswept landscape atop the hills of the High Rhön.

Right: The setting sun casts a golden shimmer over the water in the Black Moor.

influence on the countryside since the Rhön was first settled centuries ago, and mankind has left his mark. Left to itself, the region would be overgrown with beech trees within a few decades and the particular charm of the Rhön - its open spaces, vast views and broad horizons - would disappear. And thus what has been created over the years now has to be preserved. Conservationists and forest officials have realized this fact and taken steps to ensure that the gnarled, untended fruit trees and the black-faced Rhön sheep remain an integral part of the scenery. Open space is precious and must be maintained.

The fact that the Rhön spreads over three states is unusual in Germany and doesn't alleviate the problem. The traveler from Munich, Jena or Wiesbaden will find it difficult to differentiate between the Bavarian, Thuringian or Hessian portions of the region. Borders were never of importance in the late Middle Ages when the entire region was known under the name "Buchonia". The origin of the name could stem from "Buche" or beech tree or from "Buckel", meaning hump in German. The region was full of both beech trees and humps or hilltops, so both possibilities are plausible. The word "Rhön" itself is the more "recent" name given to the region; the name was first documented in a certificate dated 1228. This was during a period when imperial power was collapsing and every valley, hilltop, river and

village was being divided among the bishops and local lay lords and gentry. Borders were popular in those days and numerous fortresses were built to protect those borders. Despite its favorable geographical position and hilltop locations, the Rhön was never overrun with fortresses since it was mainly the princely abbots from Fulda as well as the prince-bishops from Würzburg who managed to secure the lion's share of the area between Fulda, the Franconian Saale and the Werta rivers.

Peasants and Farmers at the Foot of the Rhön Hills

Just how far-reaching the influence of the prince-bishops in Würzburg was can be demonstrated by taking a look at the tiny town of Fladungen in the Streu valley. Protective walls equipped with watchtowers already surrounded the town in the 14th century. Fortunately these walls have almost completely survived until the present - something that cannot be said for the majority of the medieval towns in the Rhön. Nevertheless, the most impres-

sive building in the town is the tithe building once owned by the prince-bishops in Würzburg. It used to be a combination town hall and tithe office. Nowadays it houses the notable Rhön Museum of Folklore and Folk Art.

Located right in front of the city gates is the Franconian Open Air Museum which opened its doors in the eighties and offers the visitor a walk into the past. It portrays rural life throughout Lower Franconia and it soon becomes evident that a village consisted of more than just farm houses and

barns. The Franconian villages were known for their numerous communal facilities such as bake-houses and wash-houses as well as the ever-ubiquitous brewery. One such brewery from Alsleben in Grabfeld dating back to 1836 has been reconstructed on the site. Every element of a typical farming village including the church and the schoolhouse are on view here. The former Fladungen train station has even been relocated here and a museum train runs from it on certain days.

An Intermezzo in Saxony

Following the stream-like Streu River from Fladungen, the traveler arrives in the town of Ostheim, an enclave in Saxony. The dialect remains the same and this is still Franconia but this hamlet belonged to one of the innumerable Saxon-Thuringian duchies until 1918 and then to the state of Thuringia until 1945. The inhabitants were considerably better off than their counterparts in the High Rhön and they

Left: Life used to be much simpler: a barn in the Open Air Museum in Fladungen.

Above: A protective wall around Nordheim in the foothills of the Rhön would have cost too much so the villagers built one around the most important structure in the village: the church.

Following pages: A hazy mist in the valleys makes the Rhön Hills all the nobler.

wanted to keep it that way. This may be the reason Germany's largest medieval church fortification still stands in Ostheim today. In times of war this citadel with its four corner watchtowers emerging from the double-ring wall provided a stronghold for many a human life as well as provisions and cattle. Small one-room houses and storage rooms inside the walls give testimony to more troublesome times.

The Medieval Town of Neustadt

South of Ostheim the Streu forms the border of the Bavarian Rhön Nature Park. Shortly before it reaches Neustadt, the river empties into the Franconian Saale. Even though its name translates into New Town, the wide valley around Neustadt was the first to be settled in the Rhön. The Carolingians had a palace here and there was a parish here in the 8th century. When the bishops of Würzburg set up their town here in the 13th century, it could actually be called a new town since it was laid out in grids with a large market square. Moreover, the town still surrounded by a protective wall, is heart-shaped. Is anyone surprised that this spa town specializes in heart treatment?

Franconia's Salzburg

Privately-run spa clinics dominate the slopes on the opposite side of the banks of the Saale to such an extent that it is easy to overlook one of Franconia's real gems, the Salzburg Fortress. In it heyday, the fortress stood proud and tall atop the barren hill; nowadays it is surrounded by dense woods and thus it is hard to find. The Salzburg Fortress is worth a visit since it is one of the largest commune-style fortresses ever built in Germany. Through inheritance, several noble families owned the property and they lived together within these walls sharing its facilities. Six of their establishments can still be made out. It was their job to defend the countryside for their feudal lord, the prince-bishop in Würzburg. The land in this region was worth defending because of the abundance

of salt. Thus the name Salzburg, the town of Salz and the Salz Forest. Even the name of the river Saale is derived from this same word. Although the Salzburg was in a near state of ruin by the 16th century, it is of significance as it provides a charming example of late Romanesque and early Gothic architecture.

Industrialists and Presidents as Palace Inhabitants

Heading south, the Saale valley grows narrower, yet it remains wide enough to allow the river to meander through the green meadows. The mid-19th century spa town

of Bocklet passes by and then the river serves as a source of energy for the castle mill in Aschach. The inconspicuous castle complex rises above the water mill revealing neither its unsettled past nor the treasures within. The counts of Henneberg built their first castle here in the Hohenstaufen era and the prince-bishops of Würzburg owned the property. The castle was in a state of dilapidation in the 19th century when Wilhelm Sattler, an industrialist from Schweinfurt, bought the complex and set up an earthenware factory within its once noble walls. From 1829 to 1854 potters and sculptors worked in the Great Hall in the upper story of the castle and in the kilns in what today has been turned into a park. In the end, mass-production

from England ruined the business. Mr. Sattler came up with his own house motto that has special meaning to the inhabitants of Aschach and most likely, to every house owner:

This house is mine and yet it's not.
It was owned by another before me
Who claimed it was his
And now he has been forgotten.
Someone built it and I inhabited it.
Someone else will follow when I'm gone.
Good fortune be with the man
who resides here
And is wise enough to enjoy it.

Above: A veil of mist covers the Salzburg Fortress near Bad Neustadt on the Saale River.

33

Hopefully Mr. Sattler followed his own advice as he was forced to close down his factory a few years later. In 1874 things took a turn for the better when Count Luxburg, the president of Lower Franconia, acquired the castle and began to renovate it in its original style to house his private art collection. In 1955 the count, who had no heirs, bequeathed the castle and its contents to the district of Lower Franconia and ever since it has been open to the public. Numerous elegantly-furnished rooms, old German wardrobes and furnishings from Franconian monasteries as well as valuable works of art ranging from Chinese bronze and ceramic statues to Chinese porcelain and Oriental carpets from the Far East are on display in this homey castle.

World-famous Spa at the Edge of the Woods

Many of the visitors to Aschach come from the spa town of Bad Kissingen nearby. The

attraction becomes even greater when the traveler takes advantage of an excursion tour and approaches the castle in a horse-drawn coach. Along the way the traveler passes the Upper Saline, where the Imperial Chancellor Otto von Bismarck used to reside when he was taking the waters. Even an attempt to murder the cooper's apprentice didn't prevent the chancellor from coming a total of 15 times to the spa. Politics were one of the reasons Bismarck kept returning to this elegant spa town since European royalty loved to spend their summers at fashionable spas such as Carlsbad, Baden-Baden, Wiesbaden or Bad Kissingen. Smoothing out diplomatic inconsistencies that had occurred during the cold winter months in a leisurely atmosphere could be conveniently combined with a cold water plunge and a glass of mineral water. The list of royals as spa guests is long and each year, the town celebrates its ele-

Above: Aschach Castle now houses an exquisite art collection and a school museum.

gant past in its Rakoczy Festival in which the Russian czar, Bavarian kings, Prince Regent Luipold, Empress Auguste and the Austrian imperial couple, Franz Josef and his wife Sissi, ride through the town in festive coaches and hold court in an enchanting setting. It may be of interest to know that Sissi was not a regular guest at the spa after a few mischievous boys had made holes in the picket fence around the cold water bathhouse in order to catch an accurate glimpse of her tiny waistline.

It is easy to understand why 19th century spa towns still largely consist of small palaces and stately homes. This was where royalty resided and royalty expected an ambiance of luxury and exquisite architecture. There was no statutory health insurance plan in those days either, which meant that thermal baths were ancillary to the cultural events that took place. It was a type of "Congress of Vienna" nicely accompanied by a glass of mineral water. Bad Kissingen has been fortunate enough to maintain a large portion of its architectural style from this golden age: the Trinkhalle or Drinking Hall, the Regent's Building, the casino and

the spa theater remind the guest of the days when Bavaria was a kingdom. Today some health insurance policies make it possible for the spa guest to feel like royalty for a couple of weeks while convalescing.

There was nothing elegant, however, about the beginnings of the thermal baths. The famous Baroque architect, Balthasar Neumann, and a local from Kissingen, Georg Anton Boxberger, discovered the source, later to be named the Rakoczy source, in the riverbed while they were rerouting the Saale. The source had actually been in use for a long time but this discovery allowed the prince-bishop in Würzburg to begin marketing it. It wasn't until the second half of the 19th century, however, that Kissingen, thanks to the support of the aristocratic Wittelsbach family, was in a position to outdo its competition, the neighboring spa town of Brück-

Above: This charming courtyard dates back to the time prior to World War I when Bad Kissingen was one of Europe's foremost spa towns.

Right: The Regentenbau, Bad Kissingen's exquisite concert hall and ballroom, next to the bridge over the Franconian Saale River.

enau. By 1913 the number of spa guests had increased to 35,245 annually.

The First World War brought an end to spa towns. One of the reasons Bad Kissingen never fully recovered was most likely due to the fact that much of the royalty and heads of state that had previously frequented the town had been forced into retirement and thus never returned. A record crowd was recorded in 1922 but after that, the spa business continued to decline. After World War II, the spa town was forced to rebuild from the ground up. Finding financially solvent guests was difficult due to the new border between the two Germanys. Previous guests from Saxony and Thuringia were no longer permitted to cross the new German-German border. It wasn't until the late fifties that a growing number of West Germans had enough to spare so that they could think about the pleasures of the spa waters. Celebrities such as Queen Sirikit of Thailand or Neil Armstrong later helped turn the spa into a stopover for the jet set. Yet the days of mass tourism was on the rise and there was no turning back to the former pomp and circumstances of the 19th century.

Nowadays more and more new thermal baths are springing up while health insurance policies are cutting back. In order to remain competitive, Bad Kissingen has had to adjust to the times and offer more than just taking the waters and ambiance. Wellness programs, golf, spa vacations and relaxing types of sport are attempting to keep the hotel beds full.

question of power on to Mainz. At the same time the counts were being forced to relinquish their influence, their family seat located above the town of the same name also fell into disrepair. The 19th century renovations left something to be desired but since 1952 the Boy Scouts have felt at home here in these spacious quarters. The main attraction for art lovers is the Romanesque chapel in the main tower. The tower itself is somewhat of a curiosity since it is seven-sided on the exterior and octagonal in the interior. The lower walls are up to four meters thick and it is here that the cloverleaf chapel is lo-

Between the Spessart Forest and the Rhön Hills

It is hard to define where the Rhön ends and the Spessart Forest begins. The border runs somewhere through the valleys of the Sinn and Schondra rivers but the scenery doesn't make it obvious due to the fact that variegated sandstone dominates the southwest part of the Rhön as well as all of the Spessart Forest. Let's start our wooded adventure at the point where the two hilly regions meet and where the high speed train on its way between Würzburg and Hanover in the north has turned this route into one of the major north-south connections. Here in the busy Sinn valley, the memory of the once powerful counts of Rieneck remains alive. This aristocratic family set about taking on the most important landowner in the Middle Ages, the archbishop of Mainz, by creating their own territory. Whether or not they could ever have been successful is doubtful. Nevertheless, the extinction of the family line in 1559 passed the

Above: Rieneck – a count's former fortified castle now serves as a youth center.

Right: The cloverleaf-shaped Romanesque chapel in the Rieneck Fortress castle keep is unique.

cated. This highly-unusual architectural construction houses an original Romanesque altar.

In the town itself, the Town Hall contains a pillory and a fountain built into the wall. A Classical church and an interesting Historical House make the visit worthwhile.

Lots of Trees But Little Money

The Spessart Forest starts right outside the town gates to Rieneck. Tourist guides boast of this being Central Europe's largest forested area. Despite this superlative, this forest whose name translates into "Woodpecker Wood" in English is simply magnificent. The fact that almost the entire area between the Main Triangle and Kinzig has remained wooded is due to several factors. Originally the forest was the royal hunting preserve of the electors of Mainz and the soil on top of the red sandstone was so infertile that the heart of this wooded area was one of the last to be settled in all of Germany. What was productive about forest land? The forest itself? The answers didn't

come that easily since the woods belonged to the rulers or monasteries such as St. Peter and Alexander's in Aschaffenburg. Was a living to be made from the mineral resources? There weren't many of these either. The glass industry was about the only trade that could provide a living for a larger number of people. There is still the town of Glasofen (glass furnace or oven) in the region. Some thought that robbing travelers was a lucrative occupation. The tales of Spessart robbers in the 19th century has been romantically exaggerated; not every traveler through the woods carried a robber pistol. Moreover, enough roads ran along the edges of the forest to ensure safe passage. It is noteworthy that all the larger settlements and towns except Bad Orb were located in the valleys of the Main, the Kinzig and the Sinn. Nevertheless, the scenery has changed over the past 150

Left: The crystal clear Hafenlohr River looks more like a stream as it meanders peacefully through the valley.

Above: Scarcely a mill still churns in the streams of the Spessart Forest.

41

years. Industries such as those in Lohr and Aschaffenburg have settled along the edge of the Spessart Forest. The widening of the A3 highway has made it easier to commute to the bigger cities and has brought a certain amount of prosperity to the forests. At the same time, city-dwellers have turned the Spessart Forest into a recreational park.

Heading the list of leisure time destinations is the moated castle of Mespelbrunn. The romantic setting provided the perfect backdrop for the film "Wirtshaus im Spessart", which roughly translates into "The Pub in the Spessart". Mespelbrunn was the original home of the Echter family whose most renowned son Julius was the prince-bishop in Würzburg during the Counter-Reformation. Today

the picture-book castle is inhabited by the imperial counts of Ingelheim. Guided tours take the tourist back in time.

A Pompeian Villa in Bavaria

Aschaffenburg has been the undisputed capital of the Spessart for centuries. For many years it served as a residence of the religious electors of Mainz and acted as

Above: It is understandable that Mespelbrunn Castle has served as the setting for several films.

Upper right: Mespelbrunn Castle houses a multitude of historical treasures such as this "bulletproof" vest from the late Middle Ages.

Lower right: Descendents of former counts of Free Imperial Cities still reside in the moated castle of Mespelbrunn, a popular tourist attraction.

Left: *This powerful quadrangular complex, Johannisburg Castle, dominates the bend of the Main River.*

Above: *Market Day in Aschaffenburg.*

Below: *The medieval castle keep provides an interesting contrast to the symmetrical lines of the Renaissance castle.*

a mediator between the so-called Oberstift, a charitable collegiate institution, and the heartland of the Rhine. Locals call their home "Aschebersch" and the capital looked westward until it became a part of Bavaria whereupon it was painfully forced to reinvent itself and become Bavarian. The Bavarian king, Ludwig I, made this reorientation a little less bitter by having his version of a Pompeian villa built atop some vineyard-covered slopes in the city. The mildest climate in all of Bavaria was in Aschaffenburg and this fact convinced Ludwig that this was to be his French town of Nice. In 1849, he had a romantic replica of Castor and Pollux's villa in Pompeii constructed as a demonstration of his love of antiquity.

Floor plans of excavated houses in Pompeii were studied and the result was a romanticized Classical construction, something Ludwig could easily identify with.

The entire complex of the Pompejanum is an unusual sight in Germany: rows of poplar trees and almond and fig trees add a Mediterranean flair to the landscaping. Inside, fresh and lively colors emit a feeling of cool breezes blowing. Symmetrical columns regulate the space in the rooms and decorative friezes, wall designs and floor decoration complement each other exceptionally well.

The most interesting sights in Aschaffenburg are, however, those dating back to the era of the electors of Mainz. The Johannisburg Castle is a fine example of the resplendence of the arch chancellor of the Holy Roman Empire of the German Nation. This castle, one of the most impressive Renaissance castles in Germany, was built shortly before the end of the Thirty Years' War (1618-1648) by Georg Ridinger, a renowned architect from Strasbourg. He chose fine-grained sandstone from the Main River as his building material. This local stone emits a natural, warm red glow to the perfectly

square construction with a tower crowning each corner. The old castle keep from the electors' fortress was effectively incorporated into the complex and adds a romantic medieval touch to the uniform lines of the Renaissance castle. A most delightful ensemble! Little remains in the interior to remind the visitor of the sumptuous lifestyle of the electors. Nevertheless, the apartments and entertaining rooms of the last two electors of Mainz, Friedrich Carl von Erthal and Carl Theodor von Dalberg, can be viewed on the second floor of the main wing. Whenever the electors felt a tad bored by their somewhat restrained Classical furnishings, a quick glance out of the window quickly renewed their spirits. The view still spans a bend in the Main River and extends to the Schönen Busch or Beautiful Bush. Here stands a small Classical palace in the midst of a large English garden. In 1782 Friedrich Ludwig von Sckell laid out one of the first English gardens in Germany for the last elec-

Above left: The reflection of the early Classical Schönbusch Castle in the Lower Lake.

Below left: A "Temple of Friendship" in Schönbusch Park.

Below: Ludwig I's love of antiquity is evident in his Pompeian villa "Pompejanum".

tors of Mainz. This landscape gardener went on to create the most famous of his gardens, the English Garden along the Isar in Munich.

Every detail that contributes to the overall composition of a typically English garden can be enjoyed here in Schönbusch. Long, narrow paths add depth, artificial canals meander "naturally" through the park and lead to the ponds and hills that have been created to give the impression of a mature landscape. A hanging bridge and a miniature village as well as picturesque picnic grounds and a maze are among the attractions. Decorative statues, temples and monuments abound to instruct and admonish the cultivated stroller of the Enlightenment.

The true landmark of the city is its Stiftskirche or the St. Peter and Alexander Collegiate Church. Situated at the highest point in the Old Town, the church

has maintained its own for over a thousand years surrounded by patrician houses below.

The church once owned the majority of the property in the town and was also one of the most influential property owners in the Spessart Forest. The church is a combination of Romanesque and early Gothic; it still has a Romanesque nave and the tympanum of the late Romanesque west door bears the relief of

Christ alongside the patron saints of the church, Peter and Alexander. The remainder of the edifice is early Gothic and the completion of the final chapel wasn't until 1516. The impressive church with its elegant octagonal spire houses many

important works of art, the most famous of which include Matthias Grünewald's altar painting, the "Mourning of Christ", and the "Resurrection" as well as several other painted panels from the workshop of Lucas Cranach. A Romanesque crucifix, a Crucifixion dating back to around 1520 and a portrait of the Mother of God from 1416 add to the splendor of this noteworthy house of worship.

Charitable Institution and the Old Town

The true center of Aschaffenburg is the collegiate charitable institution of St. Peter and St. Alexander. Situated on the highest point in the Old Town, for centuries this institution demonstrated its position as the largest property owner in the

Above: A drunken satyr in front of the summer dining room in the Pompejanum.

Left: A rare sight in Germany: the atrium of a Pompeian villa in Aschaffenburg.

city and one of the major property owners in the Spessart Hills. It was this charitable institution with its numerous land holdings that enabled Aschaffenburg to become the "capital of the Spessart Hills." Despite its wealth, St. Peter and St. Alexander's was never able to maintain its independence over a longer period of time. It was independent when the Swabian Count Liudolf and his wife Ida founded it in the middle of the 10th century and Emperor Otto II even bestowed his favor on the collegiate canon. Yet as the century neared its end, the archbishopric in Mainz gained control over the charitable institution as well as the entire town and continued to rule until the end of the Holy Roman Empire in 1803. The canon of St. Peter and St. Alexander's was never strong enough to fight the power and influence of the clergy in Mainz. The members of the clergy in Aschaffenburg could become collegiate provosts or the chief dignitary of the collegiate church but nothing more, no matter who was in power in Mainz.

Above left: The origins of Aschaffenburg can be found in St. Peter and St. Alexander Charitable Institution, which is situated at the highest point in the city.

Below left: Rare indeed and rarely open to the public: the late Romanesque cloisters of the Stiftskirche Church.

Right: An elegant Gothic fortress erected by the electors of Mainz for administrative purposes is perched above the town of Alzenau.

50

Although the charitable institution and the town were merely a branch of the bishopric in Mainz, both enjoyed a privileged position in the electorate. Aschaffenburg became the capital of the main charitable institution with the largest continuous land holdings in the electorate and thus the "second capital" of the bishopric. More than once the citizens of the actual electorate capital, Mainz, were a cause of aggravation to the provosts in Aschaffenburg when they tried to transform Mainz into a Free Imperial City.

In addition to the castle, it is the Stiftskirche, the charitable institution's church, that most reminds the visitor of the glorious days of the principality and the supreme dignity of the electoral title. The Romanesque cloisters are some of the most impressive in Germany and the picturesque ensemble of the entire complex that extends to the reconstructed half-timbered "Lion's Apothecary" make it clear that here lie the origins of the Old Town.

After the damage of the Second World War, the reconstruction of the Town Hall took place without taking the overall aesthetic harmony of the square into consideration. Some say this was the optical revenge of angry citizens who had suffered for centuries under the yoke of the canon. Fortunately, the interior of this Gothic structure offers numerous works of art that are closely linked to Aschaffenburg's past. Matthias Grünewald's moving depiction the Mourning of Christ is just one of many. The paintings that bring to life the dubious figure of Cardinal Albrecht von Brandenburg on his throne in Mainz are also noteworthy. His partially-completed extravagant bronze entombment in the north transept leads one to believe that this cardinal had made plans to be buried in Aschaffenburg. Perhaps the grandest memorial in the church, however, is the statue of one of the last "true" electorates, Friedrich Karl von Erthal, in one of the side chapels. This monumental figure, a dying hero who covers his head with his toga, seems to be a me-

morial to an entire epoch, the entire Holy Roman Empire of the German Nation.

Miltenberg Delights with Half-timbered Houses

The land and towns along the Main River north of Aschaffenburg belonged to the electors of Mainz. Towns like Obernburg, Wörth and Klingenberg were just as subservient to the electors as the former market town of Miltenberg. Looking across the Main from the Spessart side, the boldness of the town's location immediately becomes obvious. The waters of the Main push the town up against the foothills of the Odenwald Forest leaving only a narrow strip of inhabitable land to settle on. On the one hand, the town felt fortunate to be located on this river due to the river trade while on the other hand, whenever the Main swelled over its banks and ever the Main swelled over its banks and

the snow from the hills melted in the spring, the river was Miltenberg's worst enemy. Flooding was always seen as a normal course of events and years of protective wall-building have helped alleviate the severity of damage done. Why did the inhabitants and merchants continue to settle here despite these disadvantages? It was the staple right law of 1368 in which all the goods that were transported on the Main had to be offered for sale in Miltenberg. This, of course, was a golden opportunity for the merchants in Miltenberg to buy up goods purchased elsewhere and resell them to a buyer elsewhere at a somewhat higher price in rec-

Below: Positioned between the foothills of the Odenwald Wood and the Main River, the town of Miltenberg has no room to grow.

Right: This delightful Renaissance fountain at the Market Place in Miltenberg dates back to 1583.

ognition of the merchants' selling prowess. Life definitely wasn't bad under these conditions. Magnificently gabled, half-timbered buildings line the long main street and continue into the steep portion of the Market Square, the Chattering Hole, as proof of how prosperous the merchants actually became.

Amorbach Loved the Benedictines

The fact that several streams flowed into the Main near Miltenberg helped further the town's development. It was fairly easy to get to the southeastern part of the Odenwald Forest from Miltenberg and that provided the townspeople with an even larger market. Amorbach lies on the Amor Stream a few kilometers away and according to legend, in 713 St. Pirmin founded a small monastery in nearby Amorsbrunn. Even those who have some doubts about the legend concede that the Benedictine monastery in Amorbach is Franconia's oldest monastery. Propitiously located between Mainz and Würzburg, the Benedictine monks were able to exert quite a bit of independence by cleverly involving either the bishop in Mainz or the prince-bishop in

Left: A glimpse of the glories of Heaven in the former abbey church in Amorbach.

Above: The Baroque City Parish Church and Leininger Palace welcome visitors at the north edge of Amorbach.

Right: The Benedictines were able to enjoy their spectacular library for a mere five years before the monastery was dissolved.

Würzburg as the need arose. The monks allowed themselves to get caught up in the building euphoria of the epoch for the 1000-year anniversary of the monastery in the 18th century. Maximilian von Welsch, an architect from Mainz, was commissioned to build a new church for the occasion. Von Welsch constructed a splendid new ornate facade between the two Romanesque church spires. The interior gave even more magnificent tes-

timony to the celebration at hand. Renowned artists such as Feichtmayr, Günther, Auvera and Gattinger created a sumptuous synthesis of the arts, which makes this church one of the masterpieces of the Rococo. The famous Stumm organ-builders from the Hünsrück region built the glorious organ whose music was designed for such an ambiance. Monks haven't inhabited the abbey since secularization at the beginning of the 19th

A String of Fortresses Between the Spessart and the Odenwald Forests

The Main River divides the Odenwald Forest from the neighboring forest, the Spessart. Red sandstone has always been abundant in both regions and proved to be a useful building material that could easily be quarried from the riverbanks and transported further up or downstream. The Emperor's Cathedral in Frankfurt, the Cathedral in Mainz and the patrician houses in Utrecht and Rotterdam all owe their facades to the sandstone from this region. The locals as well made good use of this stone and a trip along the Main from Miltenberg to Wertheim offers not only scenic beauty but it almost seems as if the clock has been turned back in time as fortress after fortress comes into view: Mildenburg, Freudenburg, Collenberg, Henneburg and Wertheim, just to name a few. These are fortresses dating back to the peak of fortress-building during the Hohenstaufen period of the 12th and 13th centuries. All are worth a visit; however, one stands out due to its architecture. The Henneburg Fortress is perched on a hill above the tiny hamlet of Stadtprozelten. The Knights of the Teutonic Order were here as well as the electors of Mainz. A long narrow courtyard extends between the two castle keeps flanked by two stately apartment tracts. Although these buildings are now roofless ruins, it doesn't take much of an imagination to picture life in the fortress in earlier days. Evidence of the growth and prosperity of the fortress between the 12th and the 15th centuries was, for the most part, so badly destroyed by French troops in the 17th century that the distant owners, the electors of Mainz, saw no further need to renovate or rebuild the complex. What remains today is still

century turned the complex over to the princes of the Leiningen family. The church services are now Protestant.

Above: The thick walls of Henneburg Fortress above the town of Stadtprozelten could not prevent it from falling into ruin.

highly impressive and preserves some of the secrets of the Middle Ages.

The view across the Main from the Henneburg Fortress is of the Odenwald Wood. The Main forms a political border here and from Freudenberg to Bettingen, everything on the left side of the riverbank is in the state of Baden-Württemberg and not Bavaria. This is another example of the result of the collapse of imperial power in the 13th century and how the spiritual leaders and the land gentry divided up the region among themselves. Wertheim, once the center, now lies in the outermost northeast corner of Baden-Württemberg surrounded by the state of Bavaria. Until secularization in 1803, the counts of Wertheim provided protection to inhabitants both sides of the Main as well as to the Spessart and the Odenwald forests.

From an Illegally-built Fortress to a Youth Hostile

The Main River sets the Spessart's borders to the west, south and east and locals aware of this geometric configuration call it the "Main River Square" although the fourth side of the square from Lohr to Aschaffenburg is purely imaginary. The portion of the river between Lohr and Marktheidenfeld is relatively remote and can boast of a single town along this stretch. This so-called town of Rothenfels has only a few hundred inhabitants and is one of Germany's smallest towns. Space was scarce and

Left: Nowadays young people reside within the old walls of the Rothenfels Fortress.

Below: An official administrator from Mainz once occupied Lohrer Castle; nowadays, it is the home of the Spessart Museum.

the settlement that developed between the river and the steep slope provided room for a main street and a few rows of houses. The town is nestled below the fortress of the same name and in 1148, the Grumbach family surreptitiously had a fortress built on the property of the monks of Neustadt. The power of these monks was, however, too weak to seriously take action against the gentry. In 1387 the prince-bishop of Würzburg took possession of the fortress and still later, it was turned it into a magisterial seat. Nowadays the red sandstone complex serves as a youth hostel and convention hall.

Left: The Karlburg Fortress greets the town of Karlstadt from across the Main River.

Below: Stately half-timbered buildings line the Hauptstrasse, the main street running parallel to the river.

Following pages: On its way north between Ochsenfurt and Gemünden, the Main River often flows past steep vineyards such as these near Himmelstadt.

„Mirror, Mirror on the Wall, Who is the Most Productive of All?"

Lohr is the town where the jobs are in this region. Nowadays, traditional industries continue the long tradition of this former administrative town of the electors of Mainz. Favorably-located between wooded hillsides, the well-preserved Old Town attracts a considerable number of tourists. The first settlers on this site were more fortunate than those in Freudenberg or Rothenfels. Perched on a rise above the flood plain, the townspeople had enough room to include a church and a castle within their town. In the beginning, the counts of Rieneck resided in the castle and after the family died out in 1559, official magistrates from the electors of Mainz moved in. These magistrates were the Spessart's first entrepreneurs and as a result of their efforts, in 1698 a mirror factory opened its doors. The mirrors may not have been of Venetian glass quality but among German manufacturers, their quality was first-rate. The development of

the region is on display in the Spessart Museum in the castle. The museum also has a sobering display of the once-so-feared Spessart robbers as well as an enchanting story about a young girl named Snow White.

Red sandstone can still be found further up the Main. Not until the traveler reaches Gemünden, the three river town, and Karlstadt do the slopes change color. Shell limestone comes into view near Gambach and here is where the center of Franconian wine-growing begins. The vineyards offer an unusual geological phenomenon for the region: sandstone and shell limestone lie side by side although in truth, the older layer of red sandstone should be under the limestone. The fact that the layers were reversed results in them appearing to be side by side. The steep slopes continue up the Main forming an alpine

village of Karlburg dates back to the early days of Franconian settlements while Karlstadt was established in the Middle Ages. The prince-bishop of Würzburg commissioned a new town to be created along a road that ran parallel to the Main in 1200. The town was soon enclosed by a wall and quickly became inhabited. The increase in population at the time made it possible for the inhabitants to take advantage of certain tax benefits and the effects were far-reaching. Karlstadt soon became the second largest town in the bishopric after Würzburg. Its numerous historical buildings have been lovingly restored and lend the town a distinct charm nowadays. The Karlburg castle ruin makes for an attractive, romantic backdrop from its precipitous vantage point across the Main. The angry peasants burned down this symbol of the prince-bishop's authority in 1525. Further damage was done to the ruin in 1806. In some ways, Karlstadt reminds the traveler of a miniature Würzburg: the town on the right side of the Main and the fortress on the hill opposite.

Building Repairs and a Pleasure Garden

Karlstadt didn't only benefit from its geographic position on the Main; the surrounding countryside helped strengthen the town's political position and influence. Leaving Karlstadt to the east, the traveler soon happens upon a hill bearing the curious name of Saupurzel before entering the idyllic Wern valley. Somewhat off the beaten track, the valley remains peaceful and serene. The market town of Thüngen lies here on the Wern. The barons of Thüngen, who gave this sleepy town its name, have been residing here for over six hundred years.

Their castle is a picturesque complex of old buildings whose charm lies in the architectural diversity of various building phases. Medieval, Baroque and historical elements delight the eye.

Left: The Thüngen family still resides in Thüngen Castle.

rock garden of calve that was created by a landslide in 1784.

Drawing Board Layout of a Medieval Town

Karlstadt and the Karlburg come into view where the Main widens into a flat, fertile valley. Karlstadt is the larger and younger of the two settlements and is large enough to make it the district capital. The

Returning to the Main valley, Würzburg's proximity soon becomes evident. Veitshöchheim is one of the towns that can no longer assume the role of a mere fishing and wine-growing village of a few hundred people. What hasn't changed in the town are the 18th century pleasure gardens that the overwrought prince-bishops of Würzburg had laid out for their relaxation. Shutting out the outside world within its high walls, an ideal world of culture and enjoyment opens up. Adam Friedrich von Seinsheim was the prince-bishop whose love of luscious gardens had this blend of flora and statuary created. Mt. Parnassus emerges from the large pond surrounded by allegorical muses and the arts. Allegorical figures of the four seasons, cherubs playing and allegorical statues displaying some of the less favorable characteristics of mankind return the casual stroller to the last days of the Rococo. Take a stroll through the gardens or have a seat on one of the elegant benches. Aesop's figures reveal the dark side of our lives and remind us that moral ethics play a role in this world. Were such admonishments necessary in the good old days? Most certainly!

Left: The summer palace of the prince-bishops of Würzburg in Veitshöchheim.

Above: Only the ruins remain of a cascade in the court gardens in Veitshöchheim.

67

1300 Years Old and Still a Bustling City: Würzburg

Würzburg is Franconia's oldest city

and the historical capital of

Franconia. Its fortress, Cathedral

and prince-bishops' Residence

alongside its university bear

witness to a glorious past.

Emerging from its Ruins

Whoever saw this city in the summer of 1945 will admit that a miracle has occurred in the meantime. In the evening hours of March 16, 1945, British bombers turned one of Germany's most beautiful cultural cities into a burning inferno in just twenty minutes. Hardly anything was left unscathed and the extent of the destruction was so enormous that there were plans to build a new city elsewhere. Fortunately, a new Würzburg was rebuild incorporating the old with the new. It is true that postwar reconstruction was only a substitute for the charm that set former Würzburg apart. Yet, unlike many German cities of a similar fate, Würzburg managed to preserve the significance and dignity of its past. Franconia's oldest city continues to impress its guests. The numerous church towers and spires alone make it evident that this city's inhabitants are largely guided by their spiritual beliefs rather than commercial interests. Many have come and some have remained but all of them have praised this city on the Main. Gottfried von Viterbo called Würzburg "the rose in lush green foliage" and the author, Hermann Hesse, felt that the city was the ideal place of birth for a poet because it could furnish one with so much enthusiasm along life's path. Even the 18th century playwright, Heinrich von Kleist, gave up his life as an officer and became a writer after having discovered an affinity for this religious Baroque city.

Faith Creates a Town

Buildings are a city's memories. The buildings in Würzburg retell a tale of religious

Previous pages: Under the protective eye of the Marienberg Fortress, the Old Main Bridge connects the two quarters of the city.

Right: The Würzburg Town Hall and the spires of the Cathedral under the protection of the Holy Cross.

belief, of wars and power struggles, of the successes and failures of its townspeople, of courtly splendor and a scholarly thirst for knowledge. It began with the three Irish missionaries, Kilian, Kolonat and Totnan, who are said to have been decapitated on the wishes of Geilana, a power-hungry duchess. The ducal seat disappeared over time but Christianity remained and became the prominent force in a city that Boniface made into a bishopric in 742. The bishops were powerful landowners from the start and in the course of the Middle Ages, they became princes, even dukes of the east Frankish Empire. Their rule was religious as well as secular both in the city and in the country. Würzburg's burghers, who had risen to prosperity in the Middle Ages, were never able to turn the city into a free imperial city. Even their armed attacks failed against the overpowering

as well. For one, the establishing of the Bürgerspital, a charitable institution, in 1319. This institution helped those who couldn't help themselves. Another well-timed moment was the founding of the university in 1582. Now as then, this institution is an intellectual center and an important economic factor for the city. And not to be forgotten is the "Schönborn era". This family dynasty ruled during the building of the Residence and enjoyed a high level of economic prosperity. The city owes its gratitude to the men who made Würzburg a beautiful Baroque city: the Schönborns and the architects of the Residence, Balthasar Neumann and his craftsmen.

Secularization dropped the curtain for good in 1803. The play in which the bishop also ruled as a prince was permanently canceled by the Imperial Diet in Regensburg. The inhabitants of Würzburg were permitted to render homage to the Bavarian kings but Würzburg was quite a distance from Munich and the auspicious role Würzburg had played under its prince-bishops was replaced with the role of a provincial administrative city. The end of an era is often lamented but many are the times that the chance for a new beginning turns out to be even more promising. The citizens of Würzburg took advantage of the situation and with renewed vitality despite adverse defeats, went about redeveloping their city and taking over responsibility for its future. The citizens and the university managed to transform their former city of the prince-bishops into a lively metropolis successfully blending an historical past with a flair of modernity.

religious rulers whose authority was ever-present to their subjects in the Marienberg Fortress atop the hill. Burghers and prince-bishops quarreled often and suffered mutually. If it wasn't the plague, it was a passing army or an economic crisis that left scars on both.

It wouldn't be fair to our ancestors to reduce history to a simple matter of struggle and suffering. There were good times

Left: The Old Crane assisted thousands of vats of wine on their way down the Main.

Following pages: The domes and spires of the Neumünster Church, the Town Hall and the Cathedral dominate Würzburg's skyline.

The Cathedral Still Dominates

The center of the Old Town is dominated by neither the Residence nor the mighty fortress on the hill. Instead, it is the Cathedral that still constitutes the heart of the city. A glance at a sketch of the Old Town quickly reveals that it was designed in the shape of a bishop's miter and the streets leading to the Cathedral form the main axis of the city. It is not certain if the original Cathedral which was consecrated in 788 stood on the same spot as the Cathedral today but evidence shows that after the fire in the bishop's church in 855, a Cathedral was rebuild on the current site. The exterior of the present Cathedral is strongly influenced by the 11th to 13th centuries: a nave and two side aisles, a transept and four stately spires. The Cathedral offered more worshipping space than the town could fill. Over the following centuries, architectural changes kept pace with the taste of the times

Below: This so-called heathen's cross in the crypt of the Cathedral is one of the oldest artifacts in Franconia.

Left: St. Kilian's Cathedral is Germany's fourth largest Romanesque church.

but the edifice was never enlarged nor was it completely rebuilt. The Cathedral is therefore the ideal place to experience the history of the city in a nutshell. Magnificent effigies of former prince-bishops flank the nave. This portrayal of centuries of history in Germany is unique apart from the effigies of the archbishops in Mainz. Tilman Riemenschneider created the two true masterpieces in this gallery

of religious rulers: the red marble effigies of Bishop Rudolf von Scherenberg and Lorenz von Bibra. It is the individual works of art that linger in the memory of the observer as the interior of the sanctuary itself is somewhat plain.

Of the many noteworthy treasures inside, special mention must be made of the baptismal hidden away in the bap-

tistery chapel. It used to hold the place of honor in the center of the nave. Master Ekkehart from Worms cast this early Gothic baptismal depicting scenes from the life of Christ in 1279.

A Family Immortalizes Itself

The ambitious prince-bishops of the Schönborn family had an ornately-decorated domed chapel erected on the north side of the Cathedral transept as their final resting place. Since the 18th century the Hofstrasse or Court Street has connected this memento mori to a far more splendid edifice that bears the Schönborn mark. The Residence is the "palace of palaces", or as the famous art historian De-

hio fittingly put it: "a dream world". If buildings are representative of their inhabitants, then the Residence is representative of what its inhabitants wanted to represent. The prince-bishops of this provincial town would not have needed an architect of Balthasar Neumann's ability to provide a roof over their heads. Within these walls, the story of the ascent of a family line becomes evident; their ambitions and struggles as prince-bishops to survive on the political landscape through culture and the arts. Rarely have such ef-

ambitious new head of the church and it was clear from the very start that the run-down castle of his predecessor had to be heavily-renovated when not torn down completely. The option to start from scratch seemed to be a given when an unexpected sum of money was made available by a certain Gallus Jakob. Gallus had become a very wealthy man under the former prince-bishop due to misappropriation of funds and irregularities in his bookkeeping. When Johann Philipp Franz became prince-bishop, he threatened to take legal action against this nobleman who wisely decided to save face and hand over 600,000 guilders out of his own pockets. This was the beginning of the Residence. The new prince-bishop commissioned the little-known architect, Balthasar Neumann. The entire Schönborn family became involved in this grand project, especially Lothar Franz, also the elector of Mainz. Drafts were commissioned and discarded, architects from all over Europe were called upon for advice but one thing remains clear, this palace is the work of Balthasar Neumann. Some maintain that architects such as Lukas von Hildebrandt, Robert de Cotte, German Boffrand and Maxilimian von Welsch were influential in producing the final concept. The fact is, the 18th century liked doing things collectively and moreover, plagiarism wasn't a crime. Emulating someone else's work was considered a compliment to the one whose ideas were being copied. The dedication of the shell of the palace took place in 1744 under another Schönborn prince-bishop, Friedrich Karl. But the scaffolding was to remain. Craftsmen from all over Europe were summoned once again to decorate the interior apartments and halls to ensure that an equally elegant interior would reveal itself behind such a noble facade.

forts proved so successful as in Würzburg. The Schönborn family put a man in charge whose genius could not fail – Balthasar Neumann.

A Palace for a Provincial Town - A Work of Art for Europe

It all began with the election of a prince-bishop from the Schönborn line in 1719. Johann Philipp Franz was the name of the

Above: The Market Place almost resembles a Mediterranean piazza with St. Mary's Gothic spires in stark contrast to the Rococo House to the Falcon next door.

Italy's Most Magnificent Gift to Germany

Of all the master craftsmen called upon to work on the Residence, there is no doubt that the Venetian painter, Giovanni Battista Tiepolo, remains the most renowned. Who else could have painted the huge vaulted ceiling above the Grand

Left: The poet, Walter von der Vogelweide; the sculptor, Tilman Riemenschneider; and the artist, Matthias Grünewald; at the feet of Franconia.

Below: Matthias Grünewald may have been born in Würzburg; he was a contemporary of Tilman Riemenschneider.

Staircase? This seems like a rhetorical question nowadays but other painters before Tiepolo were contracted to do the ceiling including a swindler by the name of Visconti from Milan. Tiepolo began with his esteemed political frescos in the Imperial Hall in 1752. The first fresco is the portrayal of the betrothal of Emperor Frederick Barbarossa to Beatrice of Burgundy in Würzburg in 1156.The second politically-poignant fresco depicts Barbarossa bestowing the prince-bishop of

man Nation and owed his worldly power to the emperor.

The ceiling of the Grand Staircase was to be Tiepolo's next project and it would prove to be a far more difficult task. There were 677 square meters of vaulted space to fill; the mere size of the fresco was a great undertaking. The true challenge, however, lay in the execution of a painting that would continue to attract the observer while strolling up the Grand Staircase. Tiepolo took his work to heart and created a complete masterpiece whose individual sections were just as unparalleled. A work of art that brilliantly portrays an epoch! The theme of the fresco had been painted before in Versailles. In Würzburg the four continents naturally had to pay tribute to the prince-bishop and not to the French king. Carl Philipp von Greifenclau could hardly be accused of any humbleness! Tiepolo didn't forget to include other artists such as Bossi, Wagner, Oegg, Zick and the Auveras as well as himself in the homage. The Residence's architect, Neumann, holds a prominent place as well and in a concerted effort, these great men designed one of the first historical monuments in Germany to be included in UNESCO's list of World Heritage Sites.

The Residence's Underground Treasures Emerge

The Residence offers treasures of another kind below its surface. Here, some of the loveliest vaulted wine cellars in Germany house giant, intricately-carved old wooden barrels alongside modern stainless steel ones. Wines grown in the vineyards formerly owned by the prince-bishops mature here and stir the taste buds of wine connoisseurs. Nowadays these same vineyards are in the hands of the Free State of Bavaria and the state-run Hofkel-

Würzburg with the Franconian ducal title at the Imperial Diet in 1168. The meaning behind these frescos was immediately evident to all the guests to the palace: the prince-bishop was a loyal pillar of the Holy Roman Empire of the Ger-

Above: The putti angels in the Residence Gardens add a light, jovial touch.

Following pages: Balthasar Neumann's Grand Staircase and Tiepolo's huge ceiling fresco adorn the Residence of the prince-bishops.

ler or Court Cellars is the second largest winery in Germany. An evening of wine-tasting interspersed with informative facts about the long tradition of Franconian wine-growing can be enjoyed in the memorable ambiance of the Court Cellars. Wine lovers can relish the wines once enjoyed by the prince-bishops. These wines bear noble appellations such as Stein or Innere Leiste. Not just the religious rulers had access to this wine; the prince-bishops' magistrates received a portion of their pay in wine.

Devilish Benefactors

Wine is a serious subject in other parts of Würzburg as well. Wine-growing was the economic backbone of the region for hundreds of years. Both of the large charitable institutions, the Bürgerspital and the Juliusspital, were financed to a large extend through their wine production and trade. In 1319 wealthy patrician families founded the Bürgerspital and bestowed upon the institution numerous vineyards, most of which are still owned by the Bürgerspital today. The poor and the sick were thus aided and the noble contributors profited as well - they ensured themselves eternal salvation. One of the donors was the Teufel (devil) family and the name is still reason enough to wink an eye and maintain that in Würzburg even the devil does good work. A generous devil naturally puts pressure on the prince-bishop to do good as well. The Juliusspital is such a charitable institution founded by Julius Echter von Mespelbrunn. This prince-bishop had one of the most modern charitable facilities of his day erected in 1576. Both institutions fulfill their original purposes, both function as homes for senior citizens and as hospitals and both offer their wines in quarter liter glasses known as "Schoppen" in addition to typically Franconian fare. Enjoying Franconian wine in one of the two

Left: Although the Imperial Hall never served as a concert hall for its prince-bishops, it does provide a synthesis of perfect harmony between the hall's ornamentation and the music of Mozart.

pubs or purchasing a Bocksbeutel of wine as a souvenir is an indirect contribution to a good cause.

Wine can be relished almost everywhere in Würzburg. The House of Franconian Wines at the tourist boat landing offers a wide selection of Franconian wines from A to Z or from the towns of Aschaffenburg to Zeil. Among the numerous wine inns throughout the city, the Stachel serves food and wine in a venerable historical atmosphere within and in a charming outdoor courtyard during the summer months. Enjoying a "Schoppen" of good wine is the perfect opportunity to get to know some of the locals. Wine "loosens the tongue" and acquaintances are easily made over an a glass of "Edelfrau" or "Lump".

A Stirring Silhouette in Honor of the Our Lady

The vineyards on the slopes don't only provide the best wines, they also ensure a picturesque setting on the outskirts of the city. In which other German city do the wine-growing slopes come into view from the pedestrian zone? The steep slopes of the Stein wines and the those under the Marienberg Fortress guarantee an attractive scenic backdrop year round. There were even more vineyards surrounding Würzburg well into the 19th century. The northeast slopes of the Nikolausberg, where the Käppele chapel proudly stands and where conditions were not ideal, were once covered in grapes. The northerly slopes were good enough to produce something drinkable that could later be blended. These were the slopes that wine-growers and shepherds frequented and they were the ones who were especially fond of praying to a wayside shrine dedicated to Our Lady and erected during the Thirty Years' War. Miraculous appearances and healings occurred and believers from near and far began rather spontaneous pilgrimages to the hillside. The church fathers fervently opposed but as thousands of pilgrims were seen climbing the hill, the prince-bishop was forced to give his offi-

cial approval. In 1653 a small chapel was erected and in the 18th century this chapel was enlarged by Balthasar Neumann himself. Ever since, the black helms of the onion towers and the chapel's breathtaking silhouette have enhanced the landscape and greeted the city below. Neumann evidently allowed himself to be guided by the town's civic engineers. He knew all-too-well that the pilgrimage chapel would be visited only a few days a year but that it would be seen from the townspeople on a daily basis. Therefore, he turned the front of the chapel towards the town, i.e. to the northeast. Moreover, the fact that the chapel was no giant and had

Left: Premium Franconian wines age in the Court Cellars beneath the Residence.

Above: Stachel Wine Inn inside and out is reminiscent of Old Würzburg.

to compete with the massive fortifications opposite posed Neumann with a minor problem that he solved by giving the chapel a distinct Baroque appearance. The undulating lines of the facade clearly compensated for what the chapel lacked in size.

The terraced Stations of the Cross leading up from the town to the Käppele were also a part of Neumann's overall design and these Stations have often been described as the most beautiful in all of Germany. Johann Wagner whose putti angels and sculptures adorn the gardens of the Residence, drew up the plans for the groups of figures in the three small chapels on each of the five landings.

The Rococo interior of the chapel reveals a delicate balance of stucco work interlaced with tiny mirrors and gold leaf trim seem-

89

ingly everywhere to enhance the light in the sanctuary. A Feichtmayr brother from Wessobrunn was at work here and his exuberance is evident in his display of ebullient rocaille. Materno Bossi's use of plasterwork in the pilgrimage chapel seems cool and restrained in comparison. Matthäus Günther painted the ceiling frescos depicting the first pilgrimages and the Virgin Mary as the patron saint of Franconia. The Classical High Altar and the pulpit are later additions.

The Prince-bishop Exerts his Power

Speaking of size, there is nothing in Würzburg to compare with the Marienberg for-

tifications. They are simply enormous and the construction efforts over the centuries to secure and maintain power were no small task either. In 1200 the bishop had a fortification erected on the Marienberg hill. There were fortified walls here prior to 1200 but archeologists haven't been able to dig around sufficiently to come up with more accurate information. It also remains to be proven that a document from 706 in which a St. Mary's Church was first mentioned is actually the round church within the fortress walls. The Marienberg is the high Middle Ages in the true sense of the word. The continually growing need for protection against the hostility of the townspeople drove the prince-bishops to seek safety atop the hill.

Supra-regional problems such a quarrels between the emperor and the pope in which the bishops and prince-bishops had to take sides brought about an additional need for security. Over the course of time, the Marienberg grew into a permanent residence for the prince-bishops. The fortifications were enlarged and revised to meet the technical military advancements of the age. Neither the rebellious burghers nor the peasants revolt in 1525 could penetrate the walls. The stronger the fortifications, the more worldly power the prince-bishops attained. Only the mighty Swedes were successful in a surprise attack that gave them command of the Marienberg Fortress in 1632. The massacre that ensued is said to have cost all of the attacked their lives and

for days on end, the blood of the slaughtered was reported to have flowed out of Mary's Chapel at the Market Place.

A Zigzag Wall Keeps the Prussians Out

This defeat led to the building of more modern fortifications. The impressive star-shaped bastion trace that extends into the town was built at this time. Modern man may find this type of bastion nothing more than a waste of valuable building material and a grave misuse of human labor. At the time, however, these star-shaped and wedged defensive walls represented the latest development in defense technology and allowed the besieging enemy to be taken under fire from at least two and usually three different directions. The Marienberg lost its luster after the prince-bishops moved into the Residence in the 18th century. The fine inner courtyards and the block of princely apartments dating back to the Renaissance no longer received eminent guests. At best, soldiers performing their military service found shelter in the barracks here. The Marienberg continued to serve as a caserne even after Würzburg became Bavar-

Left: The airy onion towers of the Käppele high above the roofs of the city distinguish themselves from the massive Marienberg Fortress.

Above: Pilgrims climb 350 steps to reach the richly-decorated sanctuary of the Käppele.

91

ian. The fortress gave its last demonstration of its defensive power under the white-blue Bavarian flag. During the Austro-Prussian War in 1866, Prussian shelling set part of the fortress on fire but the Prussians were unable to storm the fortress. This final battle made it clear that, in war, a fortress located close to a city brought more disadvantages than advantages. In 1867 the Marienberg Fortress was demilitarized.

This defeat led to the building of more modern fortifications. The impressive star-shaped bastion trace that extends into the town was built at this time. The Marienberg lost its luster after the prince-bishops moved into the Residence in the 18th. The fine inner courtyards and the block of princely apartments dating back to the Renaissance no longer received eminent guests. At best, soldiers performing their military service found shelter in the barracks here. The Marienberg continued to serve as a caserne even after Würzburg became Bavarian.

Its destruction in 1945 made it possible to rebuilt the complex with a cultural aspect in mind. It began by housing the Main-Franconian Museum, the Princely Apartments and a Congress Center. The Main-Franconian Museum is a treasure trove of artifacts from throughout the region but the true pride of the museum is its Riemenschneider Gallery containing the world's greatest collection by the 16th century carver and sculptor. The stone figures of Adam and Eve, which originally adorned the south entrance of Mary's Chapel on the Market Square as well as numerous madonnas and saints carved out of linden wood are exquisite late Gothic gems. Wine-connoisseurs can follow the history of wine-growing in Franconia in the Winepress Hall. The Princely Apartments contain displays on the history of Würzburg as well as religious relics and liturgical robes. Today, the inhabitants of Würzburg can be proud of this landmark that so often in the past aroused displeasure and stirred emotions.

Left: Baroque bastions, a powerful of work of geometric art, have been protecting the medieval core of the Marienberg since the 17th century.

Where Wine Grows, Ball Bearings Are Manufactured and Knights Feel at Home

Grapes ripen on the slopes along the Main to fill the flat-bellied Bocksbeutels. The steep slopes and gentle valleys of the Steigerwald Wood and Hassberg Hills form the bridge to Upper Franconia.

The Main and Wine Brought Prosperity to the Region

Main country is wine country. For centuries wine was this part of Franconia's major export. But wine meant more: it brightened the spirit, filled the purse and provided nourishment and currency all in one. It was simple to transport wine on the river, and the hamlets, towns and markets along its banks flourished, most-satisfied with their location. Nowhere else in Germany can the traveler find such a density of fortified towns and markets as in the Main River Triangle and in the foreland of the Steigerwald Wood. Prosperity ruled and protection from the enemy, even one's neighbor, was a necessity. Moreover, almost every town was under the auspices of a different landed gentry and these noblemen had an interest in protecting their interests. Rivalry between these provincial towns was great and local pride led to one town pitting itself against another for the largest town hall or the most splendid church. Nowadays the traveler is grateful for the rivalry that went into creating the wine villages along the Main and around the Schwanberg Hill: some very picturesque old towns and fortified towers as well as stately town halls adorn the region.

Marktbreit is one such example. The town belonged to the Seinsheim family, later to become the counts of Schwarzenberg. This was their "Gate to the World" at the mouth of the Breitbach Stream. The counts invested in the infrastructure by having a stone crane and storehouse erected on the quay. Their idea proved a success and the town became a port for foreign trade. In the 16th century Marktbreit became a market town and a wall was constructed around it and its ornate Renaissance town hall. Next door, the Main Gate crossed both the road and the stream. This most unusual complex of buildings, together with the surrounding half-timbered structures is known as the "Painter's Corner". Today what the traveler describes as romantic was once a necessary evil. And, residing in such charming but terribly slanting and cramped quarters nowadays cannot be considered luxurious.

Sulzfeld, a few kilometers further up on the opposite side of the river, is another such town. One can hardly conjure up anything more picture perfect: towers at regular intervals along the wall defended this pretty wine village. Unlike Marktbreit, Sulzfeld is Catholic. This village belonged to the bishop who wielded his influence as to the villagers' religious beliefs.

Previous pages: Decorous half-timbered buildings lead to the Town Hall in Ochsenfurt.

Left: The Painter's Corner in Marktbreit includes the Main Gate on the bridge.

Below: The Market Square in Kitzingen boasts an authentic backdrop for its fresh produce stands.

Under Catholic, Jewish, Protestant and Crooked Roofs

The neighboring district capital of Kitzingen is larger and more of a mixture. The old wine trading city belonged to the

prince-bishops of Würzburg in the late Middle Ages. This prince-bishop was in need of funds so he mortgaged the town to the margraves of Ansbach, reserving the right to pay off the mortgage whenever he chose. The margraves converted to Protestantism in 1544 and even dissolved the Frauenkloster nunnery to which Kitzingen owes its beginning. It wasn't until 1629 that the prince-bishop could pay off the mortgage and begin the Counter-Reformation. His efforts to covert the townspeople to Catholicism was only halfway successful and as a result, Kitzingen remains a blend of both religions. Two stately churches dominate the skyline as well as the towers of the synagogue erected in the Moorish style in 1883.

The city's major landmark is the over fifty meter high Falter Tower with its crooked roof. Legends abound as to the reason behind such a roof. Some say that on a hot summer day the carpenters quenched their thirst on wine and thus miscalcu-

lated. Since 1967 when the German Carnival Museum moved to the tower, the roof has seemed highly appropriate.

A 1200-Year Old Tradition of Viticulture

Kitzingen traded in wine and the countryside surrounding the city is still covered with vineyards. Just under half of all the vineyards in Franconia are in the county district of Kitzingen. The region's long history of growing white wines dates back to the 8th century when wine-growing was officially documented in 777. In that year, Charlemagne gave the monastery in Fulda eight vineyards in Hammelburg on the Franconian Saale River. Oral tradition says that the wine cellars under one of the administrative buildings which was formerly a part of the Benedictine nunnery also dates back to the 8th century. Whatever the facts may be, one thing is certain: Main-Franconia has been a wine-growing region

since the Carolingian period. There were good times and bad and more often than not, a poor yield followed an extremely good vintage. Viticulture suffered most severely in the 19th and 20th centuries when phylloxera destroyed most of the vines and tastes changed as well. It wasn't until after the Second World War that this unfortunate situation could be turned around and prove beneficial to both the wine-growers and the scenic countryside. Wine is currently being grown on 5,900 hectares of land. This is a mere tenth of the size registered in the 18th century; nevertheless, the amount is considerably more than in the 1920s.

Left: The two black-roofed towers are those of the former synagogue in Kitzingen.

Below: An entire flank of towers in Dettelbach has kept the enemy at bay since the late Middle Ages.

Domina and Bacchus Varieties Become Friends

For generations the Silvaner variety was the traditional grape of the region but the more robust variety, Müller-Thurgau, has replaced Silvaner. Riesling and various new varieties such as Kerner, Bacchus, Scheurebe and Rieslaner grow on more climatically-favorable slopes and round off the wide selection of fine white wines. In the past decade or so, tastes in wine have shifted south and red wines have become popular with mozzarella, octopus and paella. Franconian viticulturists have been experimenting with this Mediterranean influence and have increased their number of red wine varieties to meet this new demand. Spätburgunder, Portugieser, Schwarzriesling, Domina and Dornfelder are the red wine varieties now being grown in Franconia.

All these varieties can be found growing on the slopes along what is known as the Main River Loop near Volkach. The entire surroundings as far as the eye can see reveal a tranquil setting; row upon row of vineyards climb the gentle slopes - lush green during the summer months and bright red and golden in the fall. The pilgrimage church, Mary in the Vineyards, in the midst of the Volkacher Ratsherr appellation, is appropriately situated atop these rolling hills of shell limestone where the sun shines just as gently. Inside the simple church, the finely-carved work of the "gentle tyrant" mesmerizes the visitor. It becomes immediately evident in his "Mary in the Rose Garland" why it was not by chance that Tilman Riemenschneider was given this nickname. The gentle but melancholy facial features of both a queen and a mother are magnificently

Left: The Madonna in the Rose Garland is one of the last works by Riemenschneider and his workshop.

Below: One of the architectural gems of Volkach is the Town Hall with its typically Franconian proclamation gallery.

Following pages: The gentle bend in the Main River is a prime example of the scenic harmony that is so prevalent in this part of Franconia.

expressed in this work of art that hit the nerve of the carving's sponsor in 1524. Riemenschneider's compassionate yet forceful woodcarvings are truly at home here between the Franconian Saale and the Tauber rivers where art and scenic beauty complement each other so harmoniously.

Prince-bishop Friedrich Karl bestowed the little-known hamlet of Werneck with an entirely different kind of gift when he had his summer residence built there. There was nothing spectacular about the setting but the prince-bishop chose this site and modeled his summer quarters after the Schönborn palace in Göllersdorf, Austria, where he had spent considerable time as bishop in Vienna. Upon his death in 1746, the summer residence and its furnishings were nearly completed. His successor, however, had no interest in pursuing the completion of such a huge edifice thus the building wasn't really occupied until 1855 when the district mental institution took it over. The large park is open to the public; visits to the inside are not advisable.

Industry Turns a Free Imperial City into a City of Wealth

Thanks to Schweinfurt and its ball bearing manufacturers such as Kugelfischer, SKF Sachs and Deutsche Star, our daily lives run more smoothly. The ball bearing industry forms the economic backbone of this former free imperial city. Nowhere else has a city of this size dedicated itself so ardently to one cause. Economic fluctuations, especially in the automobile industry, are very noticeable in this industrial center. The reason behind

Above: Werneck Castle served as a summer palace for the prince-bishops of Würzburg.

Upper right: A muse gazes at the Renaissance Town Hall from the Rückert memorial in Schweinfurt.

Lower right: St. Johannis Church in Schweinfurt is a pleasant blend of Romanesque and Gothic styles.

the city's ball bearing development is its long tradition of expertise and master workmanship. Philipp Fischer, for example, invented the pedal crank for the bicycle and his son, Friedrich, created the rotary mill in the 1880s. This was the beginning of Schweinfurt's most important manufacturing sector.

It would be doing the city an injustice, however, to reduce it to a mere industrial city. Affluent industrialists have generously donated to the arts in their hometown. The modern museum that houses the Schäfer Collection, a remarkable exhibit of important 19th century German artists, is just one example. Even though the city was heavily bombed in World War II, the Old Town still displays some of the richness of its days as a free imperial city. The gabled Renaissance town hall from 1572 adorns the Market Square and across the street at house number 2, Professor Friedrich Rückert, an Orientalist and German poet, was born

in 1788. A bronze statue in the middle of the Market Square pays tribute to this extremely prolific writer. One of his many poems pokes fun at his hometown with the play on words of "Winefurt" instead of Schweinfurt.

The Hassberg Hills or Yet Another Castle

The environs of Schweinfurt are far-reaching. Many employees make the daily commute from as far away as the Hassberg Hills or the Steigerwald Wood. This city can boast of having almost as many jobs as inhabitants. These outlying regions of Lower Franconia have remained peaceful places, in part due to their proximity to the former East German border. Much has therefore been preserved in very pristine condition. The moated castle, Irmelshausen, in Grabfeld, bordering on the former East German state of Thuringia, is one such gem. The water in the moat enhances the setting even more. The pentagonal half-timbered complex whose base is built of fieldstone, is a combination of fortress and castle. Most of what has survived dates back to the 16th century when the Bibra family resided here. These imperial knights were able to live more peacefully than in most areas of the country. This may well be attributed to the power vacuum here on the border of sovereignty between the bishops of Würzburg and Bamberg on the one hand and the princely house of Wettin on the other. At any rate, the Bibra family turned Irmelshausen into a pleasant, fortified Renaissance castle.

The moated castle, Brennhausen, also bearing the Bibra family crest, seems more medieval and remote in its park-like setting. The family line has moved to the United States and only sporadic visits disturb the quietude of the place. Two surviving fortified towers have successfully been incorporated into the quaint complex. The Bibra family was not the only line that fortified its castles in the Hass-

Above: An inviting half-timbered upper story perched on the mighty walls of the moated castle, Irmelshausen, in Grabfeld makes for an unusual contrast.

Right: Königsberg, formerly a Saxon enclave, is a true jewel among the smaller towns in the Hassberg Hills; here the Salt Market.

berg Hills. Families such as the Stewards of Wetzhausen and Rotenhan, and Stein from Altenstein, Lichtenstein and Sternberg resided here as well. They were all members of the Baunach knightly canton and their building frenzy made this part of Lower Franconia a veritable land of castles and fortresses.

The region is practically devoid of any towns; most are located in the flatlands where the roads are better. One of the prettiest towns is Königsberg. Row upon row of half-timbered buildings line the main street of the Old Town where Johannes Müller, a famous mathematician and astronomer, was born. He called himself Regiomontanus, the Latin version of his birthplace and entered the annals of history for his discoveries and calculations which enabled navigators in the late 15th century to undertake some of their daring voyages. Königsberg lies nestled against the foothills of the Hassberg Hills that drop steeply to the west and gently to the east like the neighboring Steigerwald Wood. Both are keuper sandstone hills that are separated in name only and divided by the Main River between Vierath and Knetzgau.

Where the Steigerwald Wood Lives Up to its Name

Although little of the Steigerwald Wood is in Lower Franconia, it includes some of Franconia's best appellations. These are the steep slopes of the Schwanberg Hill or the slopes beneath the Vollburg Fortress. This is where the word Steigerwald derives its name as "Steige" is German for steep path and here the paths are indeed steep. Wine-growers nowadays, despite all their technology, still have to climb these vineyard-covered slopes. There are, of course, the wine-growers from Iphofen who get to pass through of one of Franconia's loveliest town gates on their way to the vineyards. The gate to the wine village of Rödelsee nearby is the envy of every village in the region. Weather-beaten with age and picturesquely sinking into the ground, it is hard to believe that the half-timbered gate ever fulfilled any other purpose than to satisfy our nostalgic desires and decorate the labels of the local wine.

Not just the gate but the entire village with its premier wines is a marvelous example of a well-preserved medieval town in miniature. Surrounded by a wall with four entrance gates, Rödelsee exhibits the comfortable living style of wealthy farmers and wine-growers. The Baroque town hall at the end of the Market Square as well as St. Veit's parish church could well adorn and be representative of a far larger town. The house motto "wine, plaster and wood are what make Iphofen good" can be seen above many an old door in Iphofen and actually, this motto still holds true. Perhaps the sequence of importance has shifted a tad: the Knauf plaster manufacturers are one of Lower Franconia's most dynamic companies.

Left: Brennhausen Castle in the Hassberg Hills began as two watchtowers.

A Fortified Church Displays the Craftsmanship of Bygone Days

For many years this fortified church like many others in Franconian was in such a state of disrepair that no one had any real use for such a structure. Most of these churches date back to the feudal days of the late Middle Ages and were the sole means of fortification for tiny hamlets since the right to construct a wall around a settlement was usually reserved to free cities.

Normally a hamlet built a protective wall around its most important building, which was the church, and had a granary and cellar within the walls in case of an attack. Few of these fortified structures had as much charm and have been so well preserved as the church in Mönchsond-

Left: The Rödelsee Gate in Iphofen appears defiant upon entering the town but protective once through the gate.

Above: The palatial Town Hall of Iphofen's farming community was built by Court Architect Greising in the 18th century.

111

heim. Turning it into a museum ensured the church's authentic restoration and released the hamlet of further maintenance worries. During the Fortified Church Fest every July, craftsmen demonstrate their manual skills and the women of Mönchsondheim prepare a hearty fare that is reminiscent of the good old days.

Mönchsondheim is located near a hollow which provides easy access from the west into the Steigerwald Wood. There are a number of these openings through the steep slopes which prevent the hills of the Steigerwald from forming a real barrier. The Steigerwald Wood forms the heart of Franconia and the three corners of Fran-

conia, known as Dreifrankenstein, marks the spot on a hilltop where the three district regions meet and display their good neighborliness.

Left: The former fortified church in Mönchsondheim has been turned into a handcraft and agricultural museum.

Above: Mönchsondheim's lovely ensemble of its fortified church and Mesner House, which displays traditional folkloric costumes, invites the visitor to explore the past.

Following pages: The Castell Schlossberg in the fall when the golden hues of the vineyards seem to put nature in perspective.

MITTELF

Historical

MIDDLE FRANCONIA

RANKEN

Former Free Imperial Cities and a Countryside Rich in Tradition

The Steigerwald Wood in the north and the Franconian Plateau to the west constitute the hills of Middle Franconia. The historical towns along the Romantic Road offer a glimpse into Germany's cultural heritage.

European Nobility from the Steigerwald Wood

The portion of the Steigerwald Wood located in Middle Franconia stretches from the steep vineyard slopes in the west to the carp ponds in the east. The leisurely meandering Aisch River marks the border to the Franconian Plateau and the neighboring Rangau region from the town of Bad Windsheim to its mouth. The special charm of the area alternating between hills and valleys is due to its ever-changing countryside and close proximity of meadows to forests, of fields to

vineyards and ponds. Here in the heart of Franconia, the countryside also displays its humble cultural beginnings. Schwarzenberg Castle, a unique architectural structure far removed from any cultural center, suddenly appears out of nowhere. Above the small town of Scheinfeld that every once in awhile still dreams of becoming something grander,

stands a Renaissance castle enhanced by its numerous towers. Renaissance castles in Franconia were rare. As the ground on the spur of the hill was being leveled in order to erect the first fortress in the Middle Ages, dark layers of clayey shale soil were discovered and the hilltop was given its name, Schwarzenberg or Black Hill. The fortress and the settlement had several owners before it fell into the hands of the Seinsheim family in the 14th century. One line of this family named itself after the fortress and made a career for themselves in several parts of Europe from their home in the Steigerwald Wood.

Their greatest achievement was their success as officers in the service of the Hapsburgs beginning with Adolf von Schwarzenberg, who conquered a fortress from the Turks, to Karl Phillip von Schwarzenberg, who alongside Blücher chased Napoleon across the Rhine. Nowadays the Schwarzenberg line is found mainly in Bohemia where during the times of emperors and kings the noble family was one of the largest landowners, even

Previous pages: Schwarzenberg Castle near Scheinfeld lent one of the most powerful princely dynasties in Bohemia its name.

Above: The Town Hall in Bad Windsheim, one of the free imperial cities, became a palace in the 18th century.

Left: Hoheneck Fortress watches over the Middle Franconian vineyard slopes.

121

ahead of the Hapsburgs. The castle's imposing black tower is still reminiscent of its successful past. The tower was erected in 1670 as a demonstrative symbol of the family's rise to a princely dynasty.

A Country Museum Outside the City Walls

The inhabitants of the broad valley of the upper Aischgrund region on the other hand behaved far more patrician. Bad Windsheim, one of the five free imperial cities of the Franconian Circle of the Holy Roman Empire, is situated here. Stately half-timbered buildings such as the Bauhof and the Ochsenhof alongside the palatial Baroque town hall give testimony to the burghers' self-confidence in the former republican city-state. In stark contrast is the Franconian Open Air Museum just down road. The museum was founded in 1976 by the Middle Franconian District Council with the specific purpose of providing a wide spectrum of daily life, not only in a former free imperial city but also in a country village. In several cases, the

wealth and decorative design of many a farmstead can compete nicely with the homes of the so-called city folk. The museum has a representative mixture of farmsteads from the well-off farmer to the simple peasant; country pubs and mills have also found their place on the museum grounds. Even in the 19th century conditions were so unsatisfactory that many families that lived from the land were forced to emigrate. The Köblerhaus brought in from Oberfelden seems more like a dollhouse than a home for a family of four. The low ceilings, oversized rustic furniture and decorative half-timbered design make it a charming place until we realize that the family earned so little from farming that the women spent their "leisure time" at the loom to make ends meet.

Left: Mailheim Farm was moved from the Aischgrund region to the Open Air Museum in Bad Windsheim.

Above: A farmhouse dating back to 1703 next to a wine-grower's abode in the Open Air Museum in Bad Windsheim.

Rothenburg - the Middle Ages in Every Nook and Cranny

The Romantic Road follows the western border of Middle Franconia for quite awhile. The road was given its name around fifty years ago in order to emphasize the density of historical towns in the region. Starting in Würzburg, the Romantic Road travels through the Tauber and Wörnitz valleys to the Danube and from there it follows the Lech River to the foothills of the Alps. One of the true gems along the route is Rothenburg, a former free imperial city. It is best seen from the plateau on the left bank of the Tauber, from the Engelsburg, for example, where the historical townscape comes into view in the distance. It is almost magical how the town's numerous medieval towers soar above the deep Tauber valley, giving the town its name "ob der Tauber" or above the Tauber. Surrounded by the Tauber on three sides, the lay of the land made it the ideal place to build the Rodenburg Fortress which was destroyed by an earthquake in 1356. Only fragments of the original fortress remain but its layout can still be traced in the fortress gardens. The fortress was the hub of the town and the ministerial officials of the king settled outside the gate on both sides of a wide road. The road became known as the Herrengasse or Gentlemen's Road and the gentlemen became burghers. In 1274 the townspeople finally freed themselves from outside control and achieved complete sovereignty. From then on they were citizens in their own right with only the emperor to occasionally worry about. The town became wealthy due to the enor-

Left: Towers soar above the deeply-cut valley of the Tauber River. The twin towers from St. Jacob's and the slender Town Hall tower are situated in the heart of Rothenburg.

Following pages: A frequently photographed view of the so-called Plönlein featuring Siebers Tower and Kobolzell Gate in Rothenburg.

mous amount of land owned outside its walls and the crops grown there. In fact, it owned so much land that only Nuremberg and Ulm could boast of more. Moreover, Rothenburg was favorably located on a major crossroads and trade flourished. The Thirty Years' War brutally and abruptly ended this success story: first the troops came marching through and then the plague struck. The town's financial commitment to the Protestant side overstrained its purse and it never really recovered until secularization in 1803. A lack of money prevented the Baroque and Rococo styles from exerting an influence on the architecture. In the 19th century improved infrastructure bypassed the town and industry never had a chance.

Below: Two outer gates strengthen the mighty Röder Gate in Rothenburg.

Right: The Old Smithy in Rothenburg.

Following pages: The pride of the former free imperial city is the duplex ensemble of the Town Hall.

The railroad connection as well came far too late to play an important role. Rothenburg remained a sleepy medieval town until well into the 20th century when the tourist industry discovered its charm. Purists may disapprove of the year-round Christmas stores, the snowball pastries and the souvenir shops that abound but without them the town could not survive without undergoing some drastic changes. The town has passed an ordinance that prohibits any modern facades. Even McDonald's has mullioned windows and had to forego a neon sign and be content with an old-fashioned wrought-iron one.

A State of Drunkenness for the Good of the Town

The Market Place is in pristine condition and it is the hub of activity in the former free imperial city. The Renaissance town hall there is one of the finest in all southern Germany. It is hard to believe that deep holes that served as prisons are con-

cealed behind the lovely facades; Rothenburg's most successful mayor, Heinrich Toppler, was allowed to die a wretched death in one in 1408. Life is somewhat more enjoyable in the town hall's Ratstrinkstube where several times a day on the hour, two wooden figures reenact the story of Mayor Nusch. During the Thirty Years' War he saved the town from being burned to the ground by imperial troops under General Tilly by drinking three and a quarter liters of wine out of a huge welcoming pitcher in one long swallow. The

Below: A flirtatious Baroque statue in the Burg Garden.

Right: The Burgtor or Fortress Gate is the city's tallest gate tower.

"good old days" were by no means peaceful. The well-preserved massive stone wall around the town bears witness to the great degree of mistrust that was prevalent in these unruly times.

Rothenburg takes great pride in maintaining this massive structure and has to

depend on outside financial help to do so. Many memorial plaques that line the walls along the battlements reveal just how generous visitors and friends have been in keeping this medieval wall in tact. Donations have come from the four corners of the globe and it seems paradoxical that a defensive wall that once kept the enemy out is now one of the main attractions that draws tourists into the city. Rothenburg is living proof of the fact that preserving fortified walls can be advantageous. It was not, however, the original intent of the city to maintain these walls. In the 19th century the city had neither the funds to tear down the

walls nor the funds to expand them. This former Free Imperial City had been suffering major financial decline for decades since the self-righteous, staid patricians had long since extinguished any hope of economic success for the city. Nowadays the citizens of Rothenburg are grateful that decades of poor politics has enabled the city fathers to reinvent their city as a tourist attraction. Year after year, visitors marvel at the so-called "three sacrifices of Rothenburg." The first sacrifice was the custom of investing in the fine architectural facades of the city. The second sacrifice was to keep these structures and not replace them with something more contemporary. Today, the third sacrifice is being made to preserve these marvelous facades although there is no real need for many of the historical buildings, except to provide a backdrop for the millions of tourists that enjoy their stay inside the miles of medieval walls.

Left: The weak side of Rothenburg's fortifications along the Tauber River was protected by Hohenners and Faul Towers and the Spital Gate.

Schillingsfürst or the Attempt to Create a Residence and Town

Foreign territory began right outside the gates of Rothenburg. Schillingsfürst Castle is perched atop the spur of a steep hill just southeast of the town. The Hohenlohe family exercised authority here as of the 14th century if not earlier. Unfortunately their proud fortress couldn't provide protection for the family either against the peasants in 1525 or the imperial troops in 1632. A pleasant three-winged Baroque castle still occupied by the Schillingsfürst-Hohenlohe line now greets the visitor where once weapons were fired against the intruding enemy. In the 18th century a Catholic branch of the family tried to have a splendid residence and town erected on this hilltop. The location was so poor on the Franconian Plateau that even tax breaks and gen-

eral pardons could hardly lure a settler to stay. Traveling peddlers did settle in for a short time before moving on and their strange tongue or dialect has survived.

Summer Theater in the Cloisters

Schillingsfürst marks the main European watershed between the Rhine and Danube water systems represented by the Tauber and Wörnitz rivers in this region.

Above: The Court of Honor in the Baroque castle of Schillingsfürst welcomes its guests.

Right: A summer theater is held in the arcades of the Romanesque cloisters of the former abbey in Feuchtwangen.

Following pages: Foliage-covered half-timbered architecture in the Hetzelhof courtyard in Dinkelsbühl.

136

Follow the Wörnitz through the flat valley and the town of Feuchtwangen comes into view. The settlement grew out of a royal residence and a Benedictine abbey dating back to the 8th century. The abbey was later converted into a collegiate charitable foundation but found itself in the precarious position of not being able to escape its own official bailiffs. These bailiffs were the burgraves from Nuremberg, members of the Hohenzollern dynasty - precisely the authority the foundation wanted to be protected against! The foundation was dissolved during the Reformation and the margraves from Ansbach took it over completely. The Protestant Stiftskirche or foundation church next to the remnants of the Romanesque abbey cloisters still manages to characterize the former luster of the town. The Cloister Plays performed each summer within the enchanting cloisters are a high point of the town's activities. The now peaceful Mar-

ket Square was itself once the backdrop for less quiet times. The neighboring town of Dinkelsbühl raided Feuchtwangen in 1308 and again in 1388 when they opted for burning down the town. The inhabitants of Dinkelsbühl were afraid that their neighbor, who was temporarily also a free imperial city, could be too much competition.

Striving for Freedom

Dinkelsbühl is proud of the fact that it characterizes what Feuchtwangen could have become if it hadn't had such greedy neighbors. As in Rothenburg, this town on the Wörnitz is still surrounded by a wall with several medieval watchtowers that seem to protect the historical ensemble of buildings within from the outside world. The stately patrician houses with their graceful gables continue to captivate. Rarely does the tour-

ist have such a genuine understanding of medieval times in Germany as in the narrow streets around St. George's. Here as well, however, the harmony can be misleading. Dinkelsbühl had to fight hard to become a free imperial city, had to survive the town being mortgaged by the emperor and had to throw money in the claws of revengeful neighbors in order to be able to be master in its own house. This finally occurred in 1398 and from then on, the townspeople could concentrate on dealing with the squabbling within their own walls. As in most other free imperial cities, the quarrels that took place involved the burghers against the craftsmen. For example, a compromise was finally reached as far as the makeup of the town council was concerned. The situation was similar after the Reformation when several of the councilors refused to lay aside their rosaries and the use of incense.

Children Rescue a Town

During the Thirty Years' War the problem of religious belief became critical since the real enemy, whether the Swedes or imperial troops attacked, was within the town's walls. Even today the town still commemorates an event that took place in 1632 when Swedish troops seized the town: the Swedish Colonel von Sperreuth enters the town and encounters a group of children who beg him not to destroy their home. He is so moved that he spares the town.

Left: Faul Tower keeps watch over the northwest corner of the medieval wall in Dinkelsbühl.

Left: A young girl traditionally leads the flock of children during the Children's Festival in Dinkelsbühl.

Below: A row of gabled patrician buildings line the street leading to the Town Hall with its bell tower.

The Children's Festival is Dinkelsbühl's largest celebration during which children perform the historical play and receive small gifts for rescuing their town.

During the Thirty Years' War, the imploring eyes of children protected Dinkelsbühl from enemy attack and violence by taking over the role of the city wall and its numerous watchtowers. On the other hand, it was a sad fact that these walls no longer met modern military requirements. As charming and picturesque as the high walls and towers now seem, in the 17th century the city needed zigzag bastions and earthworks instead of high towers that were an easy target for enemy cannons. No free imperial city in Franconia except Nuremberg, however, had the resources to modernize their fortifications. The fate of these free imperial cities during the Thirty Years' War marked the end of the formerly successful city-republic model. These cities were no longer in a position to help themselves, let alone each other and in the end, Dinkelsbühl sent its children off to fight in order to arouse sympathy. This is the story that the Children's Festival relays each summer.

Right: Dinkelsbühl's mill next to the Nördlinger Gate resembles a miniature fortress. In the 15th century, a battlement and corner tower normally offered protection to the wheels of a mill.

Carp Ponds, Swimming Holes and an Unhurried River

The Rangau region between the Aisch and the Rezat rivers has preserved much of its pristine charm. The city of Ansbach still celebrates the bygone days of its margraves. The Altmühl River in the south connects Franconia and Bavaria.

Bavaria's Laziest River

The southern portion of Franconia consists of river valleys such as the Wörnitz, the Altmühl and the Danube and a change in dialect as well as a change in mentality. Here the borders between Swabia and Bavaria are often less than clear due to the effects of historical, political and cultural events over the past several hundred years. Eichstätt, a former bishopric, is an excellent example. In the 8th century the town was founded as a organizational cornerstone of the Frankish empire on the border between the Franks and the Bavarians. This location meant an ever-changing course of events since although the bishopric was considered a part of the east Frankish empire, it had and still has very little that would be reminiscent of a Frankish or Franconian town. During the most recent regional reforms, Eichstätt became a part of the district of east Bavaria and thus it is no longer a part of Middle Franconia. The redistricting also put a larger portion of the Altmühl into Bavaria. The upper course of the river from its source to Pappenheim is, however, still in Middle Franconia.

Previous pages: The Altmühl valley wrapped in winter fog.

Left: An archaeopteryx, a prehistoric fossil from the Jurassic Period, found in the Altmühl valley.

Above: The rocky peaks near Eßlingen in the Altmühl valley are known as the Twelve Apostles.

Following pages: Pappenheim Fortress has been a ruin since the Thirty Years' War.

The Altmühl is Bavaria's laziest river; it flows very slowly through the Jurassic limestone plateaus and through the wide riverbeds of the original course of the Danube. Thousands of years of erosion have created bizarre formations in the limestone. The Twelve Apostles, a group

147

of twelve peaks high above the bend in the river near Solnhofen, is one such example. The area is full of quarries and the stone from Solnhofen is used not only as a building material but more frequently, it is polished and used as a marble-like covering for window sills and stairwells. Ever since paleontologists uncovered the fossil mold of an archaeopteryx, an extinct reptile-like bird from the Jurassic Period, they have been very fond of working with this stone. Further discoveries are on exhibit in the Bürgermeister-Müller Museum in Solnhofen. Compared with the age of these fossils, the town's Sola Basilica, the oldest church in Franconia, can be considered a rather modern construction although some of its walls and capitals are from the original church consecrated in 819.

Encounters with the Pappenheim Family Line

The mighty Pappenheim fortress ruin that dominates the valley nowadays contains a castle keep that dates back to the 12th century when one member of the family line was a field marshal to Emperor Frederick I. This title was passed down from generation to generation and although the family owned little land, it prospered and became famous nevertheless. The "Meissner swords" in the family crest originated from the times when the family was the representative of the elector of Saxony and performed the elector's official functions during the crowning of the emperor. Friedrich Schiller, an 18th century German dramatist and poet, immortalized the family name in his play "Wallenstein."

The former Eichstätt district town of Greding lies in the remote southeast corner of Middle Franconia in a side valley of the Altmühl River. The "ing" at the end of its name indicates Bavarian origin but the half-timbered houses and massive stone buildings in the town were heavily influenced by the town of Eichstätt. The well-preserved town walls surround this Franconian-Bavarian blend and culmi-

nate in St. Martin's Church whose patron saint was the first patron saint in the Frankish empire. This picturesque town is typical for a region whose borders were continually changing.

The Romans, Charlemagne and Proud Imperial Cities

The countryside surrounding Eichstätt is familiar with its role of changing borders.

150

The Romans built a palisade, the Limes, delineating a border that was to protect them from the German barbarians in the north between the 1st and 3rd centuries. This was an area of extreme strategic importance because the spot where the Rhine and the Danube river systems can be most easily accessed lies here between the towns of Treutlingen and Weißenburg. Charlemagne tried to build a canal connection, the Fossa Carolina, between the Altmühl and the Rezat rivers near the town of Graben. It is not known whether or not the Romans had other such projects in mind but if they had, they would have been more successful in making the deep connection across the watershed than the Carolingians. The Romans' stay in Middle Franconia was shortened by the Alemanni attacks in

Above: The church stands out prominently in Greding in the Schwarzach valley.

Following pages: A fall day in the Altmühl valley.

151

259-260 which forced the Romans to retreat south of the Danube. Nevertheless, they had enough time to build the Castrum Biriciana and expand it to include a prestigious civilian settlement. A detour to this world of classical antiquity is worth the effort thanks to thorough ongoing excavations since 1890 and modern conservation and presentation methods. During the Middle Ages settlers kept clear of these ruins and settled further to the east. This must have been an important location from the very beginning since it became a Carolingian royal court in the 9th century. By the 15th century this site had developed into the free imperial city of Weißenburg. Situated along the trade route between the major metropolises of southern Germany, Nuremberg and Augsburg, economic prosperity was a given. The Ellinger Gate welcomed the merchants coming from Nuremberg. It is Gothic in style and considered to be the most exquisite example of the period. Rarely has such a defense mechanism been so beautifully adorned. It stands in stark contrast to what remains of the sturdy town walls. Water from the moat forms a double line of fortification in the south-

west corner of the wall. It was the Wülzburg, the fortifications on a spur of a hill nearby, however, that made it essential to fortify Weißenburg. The Renaissance fortress belonged to the margraves of Ansbach and even nowadays it seems to

Left: The proud black eagle of the Holy Roman Empire mounted on Ellinger Gate still reminds the visitor that this was once a free imperial city.

Above: Small Roman statues from the Roman Museum in Weißenburg.

Below: Weißenburg is still completely surrounded by medieval fortifications as seen here at the pond.

pose a threat to the town below although the star-shaped complex is now owned by the town itself.

The Teutonic Order in Ellingen

The neighboring region outside the Ellinger Gate was less of a threat. The Knights of the Teutonic Order were just a few kilometers down the road where one of the wealthiest branches of the Order served as the administrative center for Franconia. Emperor Frederick II bequeathed the Knights the town of Ellingen and the Order competently enlarged its holdings turning the post of the

Below: Spielberg Castle atop the steep Hahnenkamm ridge looks out over the Wörnitz valley.

Right: The Franconian commander of the Knights of the Teutonic Order held court in this handsome Baroque castle in Ellingen.

Franconian commandery into one of the most heavily endowed posts in the entire Order. Exactly how well-heeled the Order was becomes evident in the castle which was almost completely rebuilt according to the plans of the Order's head architect, Franz Keller, beginning in 1708. This 18th century castle boasts one of the most original designs in all of southern Germany. The flowing lines of the Baroque facade conceal room after splendid room of Classical decor. Bavarian Field Marshal von Wrede, who bought the castle in 1815, obviously placed more value in equipping the castle with the latest conveniences than in preserving the former center of the Knights of the Teutonic Order.

How to Outwit a Watershed

The southern region of Middle Franconia has never been short on history or cul-

ture. What it lacked was additional leisure time activities for the contemporary tourist. The newly-created plateau of Franconian lakes has drawn many a tourist to its shores and created an economic upswing in the region. The chain of reservoirs extending from the Altmühl River to the Rednitz has been turned into a recreational playground and yet, this is only a by-product of a huge water project. The Rednitz-Main river system suffers from a lack of water and is to be subsidized by the water from the Altmühl-Danube region. Large amounts of water are necessary to supply the city of Nuremberg and the Main-Danube Canal as well as the Main River. In addition, the nuclear power plants along the Main and the Rednitz require more cooling water than these rivers can supply on their own. This giant

transfer of water is carried out in part through an underground passageway and a series of sluices on the Main-Danube Canal that favors the Main River over the Danube. The creation of the two Brombach Lakes and the Altmühl Lake serves two useful purposes: water can be stored until it is needed and the reservoirs double as a water sport paradise for the inhabitants of the cities and towns in Middle Franconia. The projected goal is to direct around 150 million cubic meters of water from the more heavily precipitated southern region north to the Main and Rednitz. Only time will tell whether or not the Danube will one day suffer from a lack of water. The current water transfer system has proven most beneficial for Franconia: recreational facilities attract bathers and surfers alike and the

water quality of the Rednitz and the Main has improved due the larger amounts of water available during the dry summer months.

A New Home for Rare Birds and Busy Beavers

Whenever mankind attempts to outsmart Mother Nature, she as well should benefit. The heated discussions concerning the fragile Altmühl stretch of the Main-Danube Canal have demonstrated that Mother Nature also has a lobbyist representing her in the matter. The newest stretches of the canal are good examples of a change in one's way of thinking. Land has been set aside for the replanting of fauna and flora in order to obtain an ecological balance. Again, time will tell how successful these attempts will be. At any rate, the Vogelinsel or Bird Island is a positive con-

Left: Brombach Lake has become the new home of leisure time sailors in Franconia.

Above: Maritime impressions from the newly-created Franconian Lakes.

Following pages: Parts of Rothsee Lake near the town of Rothsee were turned into a wonderful ecological paradise in 1993.

159

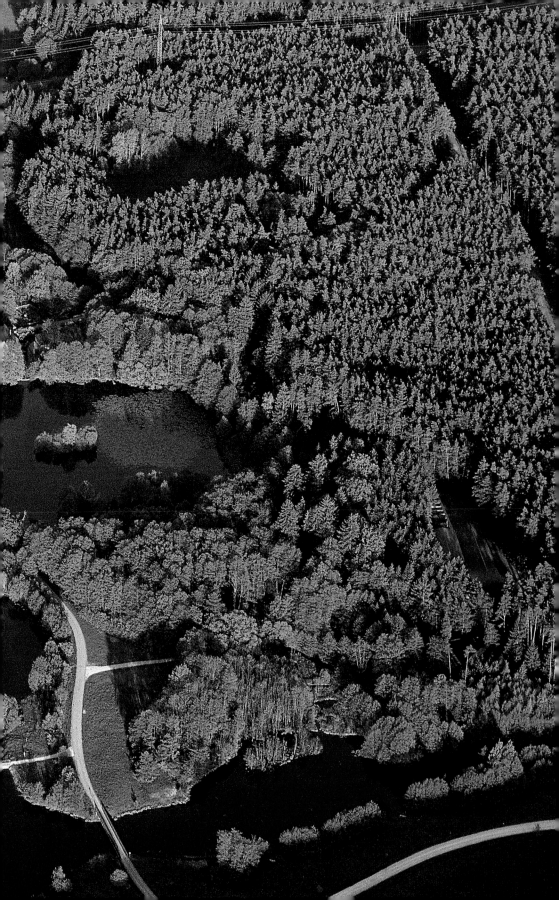

sequence of the creation of the Altmühl Lake. This 120 hectare natural habitat including the meadows to the north is now home to around 220 species of birds and some very busy beavers.

The Hops in Spalt Add Flavor to Beers Around the Globe

The varied outline of the hills of the lower Franconian Rezat River lies just north

Müllersloch or Miller's Hole in the valley. The historical townscape is delightful with two churches which belonged to former charitable foundations: St. Emmeram's and St. Nikolaus'. The two were unified in 1619. Hop-growing is the reason behind Spalt's fame far outside its environs. A good price can be had on the world market for these extremely high-quality plants with their essential oils. Over a third of the approximately 18,000 centners harvested each year are sold to the world's largest brewery, Anheuser-Busch, in the US. Hop-growing in the region was first documented in the 14th century and in 1538, a seal of approval was awarded to the hop-growers for the first time. This is Germany's oldest quality seal of this kind. The unusual architecture in the region is also linked to hops since large gabled storage halls were required for the various drying phases. One of the most well-preserved specimens is the Mühlreisighaus from 1746. The building is exemplary with its steep saddle roof divided into five sections, each story being equipped with its own ventilation slots to ensure adequate drying. The drying hall is west of the town. Wine-growing was an important industry as well as can be seen in the name of the town

Left: The multi-storied Mühlreisighaus near Spalt has plenty of room to dry hops.

Below: Hop blossoms.

of the plateau of lakes. The Rezat dug itself deep into its sandstone bed and created a valley of diversified beauty. The appearance of the small town of Spalt comes as a complete surprise. The name is derived from the German word for ravine and there are a number of such like

163

Großweingarten or Large Vineyard, situated on a hill high above Spalt and the Rezat River. Wernfels Fortress is also located high above the valley and for four hundred years it served as the home of an administrator from Eichstätt. It is currently being used as a youth education center for school classes.

Minnesingers and the Clashing of Swords

Abenberg Fortress soars from a strategic point in the Rangau region a few kilometers further along our route. It derives its name from the once powerful counts of Abenberg that managed to advance to administrators of the bishopric in Bamberg. The reason the family has long been forgotten is due to the fact that the line died out around 1200. Even literary fame has done little to keep the name alive although several German poems such as "Parsifal" or "Tannhäuser" do make mention of the family. The fortress today bears little resemblance to its original construction. Although various owners including the burgraves of Nuremberg or the bishop of Eichstätt made numerous changes, the spacious tournament field still exists as a reminder of the bygone days of knightly pageantry and the poems of the minnesingers. The era of the saga, the stories of the noble knights who went out into the world in search of adventure along with fame, honor, power and love have been kept alive in such epic poetry. One of the great epic poets of this age was born not far from this fortress. Halfway between the Rezat and the Altmühl rivers lies his hometown of Eschenbach, which became Wolframs Eschenbach in 1917 in honor of his personage. He died around 1220 and lies buried in the parish church, Mary's Ascension. Even if the poet Wolfram is not reason enough to make a detour, the picturesque walled hamlet itself evokes the atmosphere of a typically old Franconian way of life.

Below: Wernfels Fortress on a hill in the Rezat valley was once the home of a German battlefield painter, Louis Braun.

Right: Abenberg Fortress was formerly the home of the counts in the Rangau region.

The Hohenzollern Gave Ansbach a Courtly Image

Surrounded by villages such as Herrieden, Leutershausen or Merkendorf, the district metropolis of Ansbach takes on the appearance of being a true capital. The city of the Hohenzollern is very courtly in character. Margrave Albrecht Achilles made Ansbach de facto the capital in 1456 and until 1792 the capital's inhabitants shared the fate of their rulers in good times and bad. The origins of the city are to be found in a Benedictine monastery which Edelfreie Gumbert founded sometime in the 8th century on the site where the Rezat River and the Onolzbach Stream meet. Both the monastery and the town went by the name Onolzbach for several centuries until in the 18th century when the perhaps more refined-sounding name of Ansbach finally prevailed. The Hohenzollern dynasty, at the time still the burgraves of Nuremberg, first got their foot in the door in 1331 when they purchased the protectorate for the town as well as the charitable foundation. The Hohenzollern dynasty did such a superb job of protecting the town that over time it became their responsibility alone. This put an abrupt end to any ambitions the inhabitants might have had of becoming a free imperial city and although they were more than upset about the development, in the end they were spared from an adverse decline similar to the one the inhabitants of Rothenburg experienced. The Hohenzollern family had their palace built on the east side of the town which became the heart of the capital. The Renaissance ensured an especially majestic royal household but it was the "wild margrave" who first succeeded in stirring up the old town. Carl Wilhelm Friedrich might have appeared to have been wildly exotic in the eyes of the Protestant bourgeois but his "offensive" ruling style did not go beyond what a late absolutistic ruler could expect of his subjects. Dur-

Left: St. Gumbertus district with the ornate Chancellery gable.

Below: Ansbach's religious center: St. Gumbertus' Church has three elegant spires while St. John's displays two uneven ones.

Following pages: "Anscavallo" sets a more modern accent to the Residence in Ansbach.

ing his rule, Ansbach's royal household lived a life of ease against the backdrop of the illustrious age of the Rococo and much of what makes the city so resplendent today dates back to this era. The margrave's treasury was depleted upon his death in 1757. His passion for hunting and grand festivities left his descendents nearly bankrupt and yet Ansbach relives this era every summer when the palace presents its Rococo plays. Margrave Alexander succeeded Carl Wilhelm and he was left with the thankless task of replenishing the family coffers. There seems to be injustice in the world: the big spender is celebrated year after year while no mention is ever made of his parsimonious successor. Margrave Alexander ruled over his holdings in Bayreuth as of 1769 and did

his utmost as a margrave. He even rented out troops from Ansbach to the English king in order to help fight the separatists in the Revolutionary War but in the end the Hohenzollern dynasty in southern Germany failed to recover. Having no heir, the margrave signed away the princedom to his Prussian relatives for a life annuity and spent his retirement in the company of a certain Miss Craven in England. The days of the provincial towns

Right: A Meissner porcelain clock is proof that time is precious.

Below: The Dining Room in the Residence is decorated with faience manufactured in Ansbach.

Right page: The Cabinet of Mirrors in the Residence is Rococo at its finest.

were numbered nonetheless and on February 24, 1806, the exact day of the margrave's funeral in England, Bavarian troops entered Ansbach. The city's inhabitants sent pleas to Berlin begging the king to allow Ansbach to continue to remain under Prussian rule but Prussia was at a loss to defend its holdings in southern Germany during such turbulent times. The new Bavarian rulers made life a little more pleasant for Ansbach by making it first a district city and later the district capital instead of the larger neighboring city of Nuremberg.

Death in the Royal Gardens

Europe took notice of Ansbach once again when the continent's most mysterious foundling turned up out of the blue in Nuremberg in 1828. Kasper Hauser spent the last two years of his life with a certain Mr. Meyer, a pedantic, distrustful teacher. Hauser was stabbed in the castle gardens in Ansbach on December 14, 1833 and died three days later. He lies buried in a cemetery in Ansbach. A memorial stone was placed in the gardens where he was stabbed: "Hic occultus occulto occisus est" – "Here is where an unknown person was killed in an unknown manner." Historians, scholars, literary authors and film producers are still at work trying to sort out the rumors and tales surrounding Hauser in order to determine, among other things, whether he was of princely blood from the royal line of Baden or perhaps another royal line. Aside from the criminal interest in his case, the human interest is a lesson about how people deal with people who are "different" and who cannot help themselves. Throughout the city, old monu-

Above: The Orangery in the Court Garden is Germany's largest winter home to pomegranates and other warm-weather fruits.

Right: The Rococo Festival at the beginning of July brings the elegant past to life.

Following pages: The sun lures the mist from the carp ponds in the Aischgrund region.

172

ments to modern sculpture and the exhibit pieces in the Margrave Museum offer many an opportunity to find out more about the short life of this enigmatic figure.

A Worthy Residence

The Residence in Ansbach is a fitting place to rediscover the city's former grandeur. The castle, which now houses the administrative offices of the Middle Franconian government, was the design of Gabriel de Gabrieli and its long, sovereign front facade has an intimidating effect. Inside, however, the playful lines of the Rococo create a more pleasant and intimate atmosphere. Beginning in the Great Hall with its stucco work and paintings by the Carlone brothers, the visitor proceeds through the staterooms that the wild margrave called home. The fact that for the past 200 years the castle has not been inhabited enables the visitor return in time to the an unaltered authenticity that

can hardly be matched in any other castle in southern Germany. Two highlights of the castle are the iridescent Cabinet of Mirrors displaying graceful porcelain figurines and vases and the "Ordinary Banquet Hall" that in 1763 was decorated with 2,800 tiles from the faience factory in Ansbach. Castle gardens as well played an important role in life at court in the 18th century. The gardens in Ansbach are a mixture of English and French tastes but the orangery is truly French in design with its colonnades resembling those of the Louvre in Paris on the river side and a variation of the Grand Trianon palace in Versailles facing the garden. The real purpose behind such a structure was to house exotic Mediterranean plants during the winter months but in Ansbach the orangery was used as a summer palace for festive occasions. Life in Ansbach definitely revolved around the castle. Nobility and administrative officials resided in the stately Baroque edifices that line the promenade and continue into the new town while the townspeople attempted to dwell as close to the castle as possible in their homes that fill the narrow, winding lanes of the Old Town. The towers of St. John's and St. Gumbertus' add the finishing touches to a cityscape that is representative of a small provincial metropolis.

Almost all the Water Flows to the Regnitz River

The margraves made their home in the Rangau region although hardly anyone any longer uses this name, which is Carolingian in origin, to describe this part of Franconia. This is the appropriate name for the region between the Franconian Plateau down to the Regnitz and between the Aisch and Rezat rivers. The Tourist Board prefers "Romantic Franconia" but

Left: Hundreds of water buckets in the Regnitz River were once the source of irrigation for the fields and meadows.

177

this term is applicable for all of Franconia. The Rangau has numerous romantic towns such as Heilsbronn, Langenzenn and Herzogenaurach, three towns that are nestled among the rural farming villages and stately homes in the region. The word farming here does include fish farming; to be more precise - carp ponds. Carp has been a favorite during Lent since the Middle Ages but nowadays excellent carp is served in fine restaurants during the months with an "r" in them. These are the months in which carp is harvested by simply draining the ponds. The water runs into the Regnitz as does almost all of the water in the Rangau region. The Regnitz, created from the waters of the Rednitz and the Pegnitz, flows from Fürth to Bamberg through a flat wide valley that the Main River once flowed through in the opposite direction. There is no steep incline along the Regnitz but the well-supplied river has a job to accomplish nevertheless. Large bucket water wheels employed to irrigate the fields during dry periods used to be the dominant characteristic of the river. Most of the towns here keep a safe distance to the river which tends to flood the fields even without the use of water bucket technology.

Three Specialties: Huguenots, Students and Siemens

Erlangen maintains its distance as well. This city is somewhat unusual for Fran-

conia. The story is as follows: in 1686 Margrave Christian Ernst von Brandenburg-Bayreuth, a French Huguenot, settled here in what he called "New-Erlang." His design for the town's layout was both rational and practical and the new French settlers were grateful and committed to improving the town to such an extent that old Erlangen was soon outmatched. The crowning achievement was the relocation of the newly-founded university from Bayreuth to Erlangen in 1743. These two important pillars of success form the basis upon which Erlangen has continued to develop. Entrepreneurial diligence and scholarly work go hand in hand to make this perhaps Franconia's most progressive city. Proof is the close cooperation between the university and Siemens Company. One further reason for this success story needs to be mentioned. The noble family founded the city based on religious solidarity and economic prowess. The Huguenot fountain in the castle gardens is a naive reminder of Erlangen's beginnings: fashionably-dressed refugees alongside gods from Mt. Olympus give thanks to the wise founder and ruler, Margrave Christian Ernst, who is depicted at the top of the pyramid.

Below: Since 1706 the Huguenot Fountain in the court gardens in Erlangen has been a reminder of the gratefulness of the French refugees.

Nuremberg: Franconia's Modern Metropolis Abounds with Historical Landmarks

*Franconia's largest city can be
described as an modern economic
center in an historical setting.
Patrician houses nestled below the
Kaiserburg fortifications are
indicative of a former free imperial
city's nearly thousand year history.*

From Rugged Barren Rock to an Economic Power

No other city quite so well manages to represent the positive and the negative aspects of a German city as Nuremberg. The extent of power and the lack of it in the former free imperial city, the patrician burghers and a bankrupt city, the annual Christmas Market and the Nazi party congresses, medieval craftsmanship and a dying out of industry all contrib-

Previous pages: Sinnwell Tower commands a prominent position at the Kaiserburg fortifications in Nuremberg.

Left: The upper and lower chapels with their late Romanesque columns in the Imperial Fortress.

Below: Sinnwell Tower ensures the water supply from the deep well in the Well House.

ute to the makeup of a city that was once renowned as the pearl of Holy Roman Empire of the German Nation. Nuremberg's success story is the story of the people that inhabited it. There were no mineral resources or fertile farmland and no subsidies from a landed gentry behind Nuremberg's growth and development. Neither pilgrimages nor a bishop or a significant monastery attracted craftsmen and merchants who could have made a suitable living off such in the Middle Ages. It all began atop a rugged barren precipice: the word Nuremberg in German can roughly be translated as a rocky hill. The emperor had the rocky hill fortified in preparation for the expansion of the empire and as a strategic stronghold between the bishops of Bamberg and Eichstätt. Settlements developed at the foot of this stronghold and around a royal estate on the left bank of the Pegnitz River. The land was both swampy and sandy and the inhabitants alone had to surmount this problem. The only bit of outside help was derived from the fact that during this period trade routes were being improved

within the Holy Roman Empire and the hub of the empire, originally in the western part of Germany, was moving eastwards due to new colonization. Nuremberg suddenly found itself in its heart along major trade routes. As early as the 13th century the desire for economic prosperity, an innovative spirit and merchants willing to take great risks formed the backbone of the city. The Hohenstaufen dynasty and later the emperors from the Luxembourg dynasty considered Nuremberg to be the center of their empire and their demands were fulfilled accordingly. In such an environment the city was not only able to become a free imperial city but also to finally rid itself of the power-hungry burgraves. Nuremberg flourished in the 15th and 16th centuries. At this time it was one of the most densely-populated German-speaking cities in the empire and the export of precision products as well

Right: A view of the Kaiserburg and the Dürer House in Old Nuremberg.

Below: Tiergärtnertor Square is a favorite meeting place in the Old Town during the summer months.

as swords and armor brought such wealth to the burghers that they were able to commission great artists such as Albrecht Dürer, Adam Kraft, Veit Stoß and the Vischer brothers. None of these men could complain of a lack of work. The time came, however, when the burghers became more selfish in their personal desires and had stately homes built in the neighboring countryside for weekend excursions. Affluence does not only make a man rich, it can also make him indolent.

The Decline Ended in Bavaria

It was often the case that Nuremberg reacted far too slowly to changing circumstances. One of its problems was that it had no well-rounded economic hub. It is true that the free imperial city owned more property than any other such German city, yet the area was too small to be financially viable. This was fatal for a city whose existence depended on exports whose prices were far less competitive after tariffs and customs. Nuremberg was not alone in its misery; the situation was similar in other free imperial cities as well. The heydays of the free imperial cities had become passé and the future belonged to the large princely dynasties. The final blow came during the Thirty Years' War (1618-1648) which put an end to existing trade relations and astronomical sums had to be paid out to friend and foe. The huge number of deaths meant a shrinking market and Nuremberg found itself over seven million guilders in debt. During the next 150 years the city failed to recapture its independence and former prosperity. The 18th century was therefore a modest century. Not much was built

except for two churches; thus the city maintained its late medieval character even if bay windows were being added to the houses in the narrow streets to satisfy the curiosity of the dwellers. The city's inhabitants were not exactly thrilled to become a part of the Catholic state of Bavaria in 1806 even though this meant the opportunity for an economic upswing since anything was better than being led around by the nose and exploited by disinterested patricians.

Diligence Leads to Affluence

After 1806 Nuremberg was again in a position to roll up its sleeves and prove that it still had the potential it so ably demonstrated as a free imperial city. In a matter of a few years, Nuremberg became Bavaria's leading industrialized city. It is not an accident that in 1835 Germany's first train traveled from Nuremberg to Fürth. The population grew from 25,000 to 330,000 between 1810 and 1910. Entrepreneurs like Theodor von Cramer-Klett, Lothar Faber and Sigmund Schuckert founded MAN, Faber-Castell and Siemens-Schuckert in Nuremberg. The transformation from a city of craftsmen, merchants and patricians to a city of leading European companies and a productive workforce was complete. Fortunately, industrialization did not penetrate the medieval walls of the well-preserved Old Town which remains an old Franconian gem despite the distant smokestacks and workers' housing.

Left: The half-timbered buildings in Weißgerbergasse or Tanner's Street are an authentic example of medieval Nuremberg.

Following pages: Prophets and rulers assemble at the Beautiful Fountain on the Market Square in Nuremberg. Our Lady's Church can be seen in the background.

A Thousand Years of History End in Rubble and Ashes

The more influential the city became, the more socialist it became. The fact that Nuremberg provided the setting for the largest Nazi party congresses had actually nothing to do with the political power in the city. Nuremberg, the former heart of the Holy Roman Empire, was the perfect backdrop for Hitler's nascent Third Reich. After the German occupation of Austria, the Crown Jewels were even brought back to Nuremberg. The ambitious senior Nazi party official in Franconia and editor of an anti-Semitic Nazi party official newspaper, Julius Streicher, seemed to be the ideal instrument to car-

ninety percent of the historical buildings were reduced to rubble. After the war, great efforts were taken to rebuild a new city oriented on the richness and charm of the old medieval one.

The City's Landmark – the Kaiserburg

The Emperor's Fortress or Kaiserburg soars proudly above the city streets as it has for as far back as can be remembered. It is

Left: The world famous Christkindl Christmas Market is located between the Beautiful Fountain and Our Lady's Church.

Below: Each Advent, a young girl trades in her jeans for a long, white dress to open the Christkindl Market from the balcony of Our Lady's Church.

Far below: The famous Nuremberg "Zwetschgenmännla" or little, dried prune figures.

ry out party policy. The former grounds of the Nazi party congresses still pose a heavy burden on the citizens of this city in as far as to how to deal with and learn from this not-so-distant past. Just as tragic were the numerous bombs that destroyed the historical heart and soul of the city between 1942 and April 16, 1945. Only a handful of German cities were as severely bombed as Nuremberg where

hard to believe that this fortified complex once housed three rulers - the emperor, the burgraves and the burghers of Nuremberg. The fortress is more or less a symbol of the Holy Roman Empire of the German Nation with all of its advantages and drawbacks. A breath of Old Nuremberg can be felt in the narrow streets at the foot of the fortress at the Tiergärtner Gate. The house that Albrecht Dürer lived in is one of the charming medieval buildings here. Known as Germany's "Renaissance Man," in around 1500, Dürer set about turning the city into a city of muses. Nuremberg's Market Square is the only large square located between the city's two main churches, St. Sebald's and St. Lorenz's. The Christkindl Christmas Market is held every year during Advent

between the 19-meter high filigree Schöner Brunnen or Beautiful Fountain from the 14th century and the Frauenkirche or Our Lady's Church.

Disgraceful Trinkets and Dried Plum Figures

Naturally Christkindl (an angel with long golden locks) officially opens the market from the balcony of the Frauenkirche where she proclaims in the local dialect that there is hope that the city will continue to serve bratwurst and gingerbread after the Resurrection. The current Christkindl Christmas Market dates back to 1933 when a tinsel angel officially opened the market. The Christmas Market had previously been held in

various places including the dismal, empty Transportation Museum. In hopes of rejuvenating local craftsmanship during the winter, this market held during Advent offered numerous opportunities to earn a little extra and to try out new products on the locals as well as sell the world famous Nuremberg "Tand," the name for typical, local products such as glass beads, costume jewelry and mirrors. Unfortunately, such good intentions led to including some less than desirable lewd trinkets and on Christmas Eve in the year 1610, local councilmen confiscated "disgraceful, painted wooden objects" from a wood turner by the name of Entner. Just what these bawdy woodcuts represented was never recorded but their popularity was so immense that in

1649 the council issued a special decree against the sale of "lewd and disgraceful objects" at the market.

Nowadays, the visitor can enjoy a glass of hot mulled wine, gingerbread-like Lebkuchen and Zwetschgenmännla (little prune men). And, one other thing has changed since the pre-Reformation: gift-giving is no longer on New Year's Day or Epiphany.

Above: Weinstadel, a former pub, a water tower and Hangman's Footbridge are reflected in the river Pegnitz that divides the Old Town.

An "Angelic Salutation" Moves the Soul

In order to get a glimpse of the city's artistic development during its prime, a visit to the parish churches is a must. Especially St. Lorenz's presents itself as a cultural treasure house. Innumerable late Gothic altars bear witness to both the wealth of prosperous donors as well as their desire to enter Heaven's Gates. One had to take the necessary precautions to be prepared for Judgement Day. Be that as it may, Veit Stoß's "Angelic Salutation" medallion and Adam Kraft's remarkable slender stone tabernacle have been attracting both the pious and art lovers for approximately 500 years.

Because Nuremberg was neither a bishopric nor had any special local saints to honor, its burghers devoted all their energy to building and decorating their two main parish churches. This made sound economic sense due to the simple fact

that in the Middle Ages, a functioning religious infrastructure played an important role. After all, what good was an earthly fortune when it couldn't be used to ensure a place in the heavenly kingdom? Eternity lasted far too long to spend all one's time in Purgatory or Hell.

Fortunately, the iconoclastic Reformation never made it to Nuremberg; both parish church interiors still evoke the atmosphere of the late Middle Ages. Besides, iconoclasm has no place in a Franconian soul; no one would think of tossing out an object that had once cost an enormous sum. One just never knows when it might become useful…

Left: The self-assured sculptor, Adam Krafft, bears the weight of his over 20-meter high tabernacle in St. Lorenz's.

Above: For over 500 years, the angel Gabriel has been bringing the annunciation to the Virgin Mary in Veit Stoss' "Angelic Salutation" in St. Lorenz's.

Right: The Gothic rose window in St. Lorenz's Parish Church.

Following pages: The slim spires of St. Sebald's share the skyline with the Imperial Fortress.

The Land of Garlic, Imperial Forests and Stately Homes in the Regnitz Valley

Nuremberg's neighbors were both hard-working and leisurely. Business went hand in hand with stately country homes. Jagged walls of rock line the valley of the Franconian Alb Plateau.

Germany's First Train Destination – Fürth

At the mention of Nuremberg, the city of Fürth immediately comes to mind since Germany's first train line connected these two cities. The inhabitants of Fürth have got used to the fact that their city lies close to Nuremberg and not the other way round even though at one time the possibility did exist. Fürth is doubtlessly the older of the two settlements and enjoyed market privileges as early as 1062. The town was also favorably located at the confluence of the Pegnitz and Rednitz rivers. The city's three rulers kept the town from developing as auspiciously as its neighbor. The constant bickering carried out among Bamberg's bishop, the burgrave from Nuremberg and the free imperial city of Nuremberg itself prevented the flourishing of Fürth. Not until Nuremberg's power was cut off in the 18th century could Fürth begin to prosper eco-

nomically. What wasn't permitted in Nuremberg was attempted in Fürth - usually successfully - which resulted in the city's rapid growth. The fact that Fürth was spared any major bomb damage during the Second World War makes it the best place in Franconia to study 19th century architectural development. The rapidness of the city's growth is documented in its various representative buildings. The Town Hall has a tower that rivals none other than the Palazzo Vecchio in Florence while the local theater was designed by Europe's leading theater architects of the era, Fellner & Helmer, from Vienna. This extravagance was made possible through the generous contributions of the citizens of Fürth in 1902. Over half of the donations came from the Jewish

Previous pages: The Schwarach River, which isn't much wider than a stream, has managed to gnaw a pretty ravine out of the sandstone rock.

Above: Neunhof Castle in the Land of the Garlic Bulb is a typical patrician stately home.

Right: The Town Hall in Fürth might seem more at home in Tuscany.

community who had been influential in the city since the 17th century making it one of the most notable Jewish communities in Germany. Fürth was the home of men such as the publisher, Ullstein, the author, Wassermann, and the former Secretary of State of the US, Henry Kissinger. This community like so many others fell victim to the Nazi idea of racial purity. The reputation Fürth had enjoyed as a city of tolerance quickly disappeared after the Nazi seizure of power.

Diligent Asylum-seekers

How economically-influential the arrival of a persecuted people can be is demonstrated in the town of Schwabach, the most southerly edge city of Nuremberg. The beginnings date back to the 14th century when Nuremberg deported metalworkers who then settled down in Fürth. Later the town took in a good two hundred Austrian Protestants and at the end

Above: The Town Hall, parish church and fountain delight the eye at Schwabach's Market Square.

Right: The Golden Roof of the bay window of the Town Hall gives testimony to the long goldsmith tradition in Schwabach.

of the 17th century, Protestant Huguenots broadened the range of merchandise to include carpets and stockings. The margraves profited from having such craftsmen in their town; Schwabach soon became their greatest source of taxation and the first early industrial center. The heart of the city looks anything but industrial. Ornately-decorated half-timbered buildings flank the narrow streets and the main square, the Königsplatz or King's Square, is surrounded by a uniform ensemble of historical buildings. The Schöner Brunnen or Beautiful Fountain stands in the middle of the square and since 1717 the eagle perched at the top has been declaring that the ruler of the city stems from the noble Brandenburg-Ansbach line. The Town Hall on the eastern side of the square continues to fascinate the observer with its highly-decorative bay window and golden roof. The reputation of the goldsmiths from Schwabach was widespread; these were true craftsmen in the art of gold leaf.

Where Patricians Spent their Leisure Time

The countryside surrounding Nuremberg is scattered with stately patrician homes. Whether it be in the Land of the Garlic Bulb, at the edge of the Sebald and Lorenz Imperial Forests or in the Pegnitz valley, historic houses with steep-gabled roofs situated in park-like settings abound. The

Left: Carpenters added a bell tower to the rugged stone hewn tower in Hohenstein.

Above: Hohenstein Fortress, high above Sittenbach valley, was formerly a Bavarian outpost.

natural desire to escape the crowded conditions within a walled city began in the late Middle Ages when the well-heeled converted houses surrounded by a pond into small castles with corner towers. Originally these castles did serve as a type of preemptive line of defense for the city. As the homes became more luxurious however, they were turned into summer residences or hunting lodges. A pristine example is Neunhof Castle in the Land of the Garlic Bulb. The castle today still closely resembles the one the Kress family refurbished and enlarged in 1525. The geometrically laid-out Baroque garden was added later. The fine decor of the Great Hall and especially the decor of the kitchen - one so fine that it would be a shame to actually use it - along with the chapel are typical for a weekend cottage occupied by Nuremberg's high society during the Renaissance.

The Usefulness of Woods and Water

The environs around Nuremberg were more than just a leisure park for the city's patricians. They were an essential part of the economy of the free imperial city as well. Even the large imperial forests were utilized and were some of the earliest examples of woodland management in Europe. Apart from felling trees to fulfill the

great need for wood, the forests were where the beekeepers kept their hives. The honey was used as a basic sweetener and the sole sweetener for the Nuremberg specialty Lebkuchen or gingerbread. The Pegnitz River was put to use as well; it was the source of water power for the numerous iron forges that were established during the 16th and 17th centuries and still in operation during the Industrial Revolution. Not until the area where the Pegnitz valley grows more narrow and the rocky slopes come into view is the countryside allowed to be just that - scenic beauty. Beyond Hersbruck begins the region known as the Hersbrucker Schweiz distinguished by rock formations from the Jurassic Period. This area also belonged to Nuremberg after the free imperial city conquered it during the War of Landshut Succession and received confir-

Left: The setting sun turns the high Hersbruck plateau into a stage of natural scenic beauty.

Above: Idyllic Lungsdorf lies in the peaceful Pegnitz valley on a trout stream surrounded by rocky crags.

mation of possession in 1521. Nevertheless, the villages in this region did not grow as a visit to Vorra and Lungsdorf will confirm. Moreover, the patricians and nobility from Nuremberg were not attached to the region and thus never built any stately homes here. Instead, fortresses or fortress ruins dominate the deeply-grooved rocky hilltops. Hohenstein Fortress is perched atop the highest point in Middle Franconia at 634 meters. The fortress was used for administrative purposes from the very start; a bailiff or administrator represented the interests of his sovereign, which was the Nuremberg City Council as of 1505. Beforehand, the fortress had belonged to the Bavarian dukes and served as a demonstration of their ambitions in the northern border territory. Veldenstein Fortress in the upper Pegnitz valley is another example of the keen interest in this region. The bishop of Bamberg had this fortress enlarged in order to have more control over the border to his territory. By the time of the Thirty Years' War, improved siege techniques and artillery left the fortress obsolete and at various times, soldiers from Brandenburg

and Nuremberg as well as the Swedes all seized Veldenstein. It is easy to imagine how the mercenaries went through the fortress with a fine-toothed comb searching for treasures to improve their poor soldier's pay. These mercenaries were just as unsuccessful as the American troops in 1945 when they systematically went through the fortifications with pneumatic drills to try to uncover the hidden treasures of Hermann Göring. Göring, the "Reich's professional hunter" had bought the complex in 1939 as a hunting lodge. The only booty the Americans found was a case containing wine, champagne and cognac. Nowadays a glass of wine or champagne is much easier to come by since a part of the fortress has been converted into a hotel.

Above: The sovereign prince-bishops of Bamberg displayed their power for over 800 years from Veldenstein Fortress located above the town of Neuhaus on the Pegnitz.

OBERFR

scenic
UPPER FRANCONI

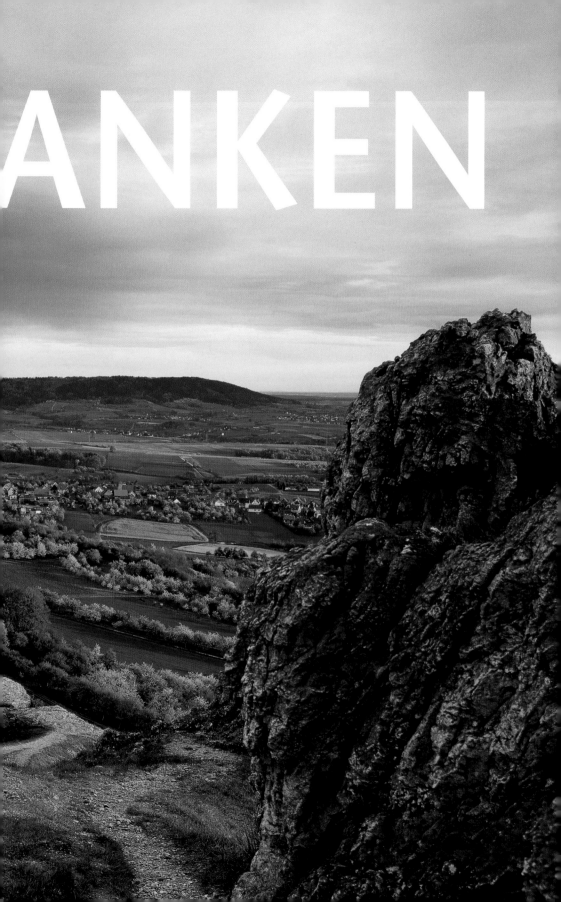

ANKEN

Forests Atop Rocky Outcrops and Palaces Nestled in the Hills

The breathtaking rugged rocky valley of Franconian Switzerland makes the heart beat faster. The Steigerwald Wood is far gentler in appearance and Bamberg is a World Heritage Site.

German Romantics Take to the Hills

"... it's a region that makes one swoon a thousand times," were the words of the German Romantic poet, Ludwig Tieck, in 1793 upon his return from a trip over Pentecost with his student friend, Wilhelm Wackenroder, from Erlangen to the Muggendorf Hills. The untamed rocky cliffs, the fortresses perched atop precipitous spurs, the clear streams and the unspoiled nature of the villages released a huge amount of enthusiasm in both poets - enthusiasm that still prevails two hundred years later. Ever since the Romantics began to discover beauty in the bizarre and unusual as well as the picturesque, the Wiesent, Püttlach or Ailsbach

valleys have become a type of "Schweiz" or Switzerland and the region isn't viewed as merely being some remote area where farmers struggle to make a living off their small plots of land. The Romantics set new standards that are still valid. We have become a leisure time society that instead of doing hard physical labor in a field in order to make ends meet, uses up its extra energy by working out in an overheated fitness center. From this point of view,

the scenic beauty of Upper Franconia can be enjoyed as a free time activity.

Franconia's "Switzerland" and Other Provincial Regions

This region between Forchheim and Bayreuth is known as "Schweiz" or Switzerland in English but it does not get its name from the people who settled here. The inhabitants couldn't pay in Swiss francs either even though the name might imply such. Being called "Schweiz" has been considered an honor since the 19th century when the scenic beauty of this area was first compared to Switzerland, the non plus ultra of natural beauty. The Franconian version, however, is made up of dyed-in-the-wool Franconians like the inhabitants of Streitberg or Pottenstein and these people as well were heavily influenced by the individual power exerted by the various provincial towns. As a result, beginning in the Middle Ages, rarely a prominent rocky

Previous pages: The town of Pottenstein is nestled in the rugged rocky valley; Pottenstein Fortress stands at the edge of the precipice above the town.

Left: Stalagmites and stalactites almost meet in Bing Cave.

Above: The hazardously perched rocks give this region its name: Franconian Switzerland.

outcrop was without some sort of fortification. Nowadays the traveler enjoys these charming ruins that fit so perfectly into the landscape; originally they were built to demonstrate authority. Pottenstein Fortress is where the bishops of Bamberg triumphed over the neighboring nobility: the margraves of Bayreuth, the Schlüsselberg family line or the burghers of the free imperial city of Nuremberg. The fortress was an unequivocal sign of where the borders lay. The Countess of Thuringia, Elisabeth, was the best-known guest at the fortress although her visit was anything but voluntary. She arrived in 1228 to escape the fury of her in-laws. Her charitable disposition throughout her life was the cause of their hatred towards her. Be that as it may, she was beatified after her death.

Stone Created Drop by Drop

It takes a great amount of time for stalagmites like the "Millionaire" in Sophie's

Cave to be worthy of such a name. First of all, water has to carve out the caves from the porous limestone in order for the billions upon billions of drops of carbonate of lime to form such splendor. Geologically, these are the Franconian Jurassic Hills, the northern continuation of the large European Jurassic Mountains that begin in the French West Alps and continue across the French and Swiss Jurassic Mountains to the Swabian Alb near Stuttgart, ending with the hills between Bamberg and Bayreuth. Deposits from a primordial ocean allowed tremendous layers of limestone to form and mold stream and river valleys as well as subterranean caves. Most of Germany's caves are

Above: Tüchersfeld in the Püttlach valley is an unusual blend of man and nature.

Left: The Bavarian king, Ludwig I, was enchanted by Rabenstein Fortress.

Following pages: Gößweinstein Fortress brings 19th century Romanticism back to life.

to be found in Franconian Switzerland and the Swabian Alb. Franconian Switzerland alone is said to have over 1000 smaller and larger caves. The most enchanting and easily accessible are Bing Cave, Teufelshöhle or Devil's Cave and Sophie's Cave. These caves once provided shelter for our ancestors.

A Fortress on Every Rocky Crag

Medieval man saw these rocky reefs as the ideal spot to effectively demonstrate his right to power. Rabenstein Fortress in the Ailsbach valley is a symbiosis of rock and architecture. The fortress, which underwent almost complete renovation in the 19th century, emerges from the rock as an impregnable stronghold above the meandering valley. As if this rugged scenery needed any manmade showpiece! The numerous fortresses in this remote, thinly-populated region were not built for military defense purposes. Instead, they served as messengers whose words were clear: "Here I am. If it doesn't suit you, then you will have to drive me out!" It was therefore possible for several noble families to maintain their in-

Left and above: The Neideck Ruin soars in the distance from the Wiesent valley between Streitberg and Muggendorf.

221

dependence in this region - the topography was indeed very favorable.

How Nicely a Pub and a Museum Can Complement Each Other

The most unusual sight in the Püttlach valley in the heart of Franconian Switzerland is the craggy village of Tüchersfeld. There were once two fortresses here and after the lower one was destroyed, Jews from Bamberg settled here. The so-called Jewish Cemetery has been the home of the unique Franconian Switzerland Museum since 1985. Topography, geology, Jewish history and official documents as well as handicrafts and the rural way of life are well-documented in this worthwhile museum. The visitor learns of the daily frustrations as well as the celebrations of his forefathers. About the only thing the museum doesn't provide is culinary delights. Not to worry since this region has long been famous for its hearty, nutritious cuisine and the innumerable regional inns and pubs offer a wide variety of everything baked, roasted, brewed and distilled: dishes like spareribs and dumplings or fresh river trout in every imaginable variation. A half liter of beer to wash it down and you are one of the locals. No other region in Germany abounds with so many breweries as Upper Franconia. There are still around 300 in the environs of Bamberg alone! And, a large number of them are in Franconian

Switzerland. It is often maintained that there are as many caves here as types of beer. Which other region can boast the likes of such!

A Friend of God's Builds a Fortress

Let's retreat from the culinary and return to the well-fortified. The pilgrimage town of Gößweinstein lies high above a cobweb of narrow valleys known as Behringer Mill. The miracle-working image of the Holy Trinity in the 18th century Baroque church draws devout pilgrims into the sanctuary while art lovers are attracted by the name of the magnificent church's ar-

Above: Ludwig Cave has ice-covered stalagmites and stalactites in the winter.

Left: Little more than a rocky pedestal remains of the once impressive Streitburg Fortress above the Wiesent valley.

chitect, Balthasar Neumann. There is also something for the fortress enthusiast since the highest peak in the town has had a fortress on it since the 11th century. The bishop of Bamberg invested a certain Count Goswin, whose name translates into friend of God's, with this land. Eight hundred years later the fortress was to be the musical inspiration for the Castle of the Holy Grail in Parsifal. Although Richard Wagner sojourned quite often in the then newly-renovated fortress, the musical inspiration story is nothing more than a rumor. Medieval surroundings did not provide sufficient inspiration for the great genius from Bayreuth!

Where the Ravages of Time Gladly Gnaw

The same valley but another fortress. This time it is the Neideck Ruin and the question may not remain unanswered as to why so many of these, for the most part

very remote fortresses, have remained empty for so many generations. Various wars such as the Hussite War in the 15th century, the Peasants' War in the 16th or the Thirty Years' War in the 17th century destroyed almost every fortress at least once. Without a concrete reason to have a fortress in the region, rebuilding of such a stronghold was not an option. Neideck was destroyed during the Second Margraves War in the 16th century and the fact that the fortress was little more than an administrative outpost, meant that it was more convenient to build a completely new one in the valley. What remained as a ruin fell victim to economic greed in the 18th century when marble-like limestone was discovered and quarried on the site. This stone was transported to Würzburg to decorate the Imperial Hall in the Residence. The rocky outcrop and the ruin were once one and they were both of stone. Just as years of erosion can destroy a gigantic hillside until only a remnant remains, this ruin is likewise a remnant of a once bold human project. This

Above: The castle and church in Egloffstein share the narrow space atop a steep rocky cliff overlooking the Trubach valley.

Below: Year after year the barren summit of the Ehrenbürg celebrates Franconia's highest Church Dedication Day.

is what the German Romantics loved about these undertakings of human arrogance: they bear witness to the fact that in view of the endless cycles of nature, mankind's work can only be considered ephemeral.

The Hill Calls on Walpurgis Night

Approaching Franconian Switzerland from the west, Walberla Hill offers the most spectacular prelude to the valleys of the region. The natural landmark's prominent summit of bright gray stone and its lush green meadows greet the traveler from afar. The Celts had an extensive, almost urban hillfort here as of around 1000 BC. We know practically nothing about the inhabitants but archeologists have excavated unusual finds that point to the extensive trade relations of these "citizens" of the hill. A small perfume flask from Greece and amber from the Baltic Sea region give an indication of the lifestyle these people were accustomed to.

If once again in a few hundred years archeologists should happen to excavate the Ehrenbürg, this plateau with two peaks, they are bound to find artifacts of an entirely different nature. At least as far

back as 1360 people have gathered on this hilltop to celebrate the anniversary of the hill's patron saint, Walburga, year after year. In the 20th century this annual festivity known as Walpurgis Day was fixed on the first Sunday in May and there is no lack of enthusiasm for one of Germany's most popular and promising celebrations. Moreover, when the spring winds blow propitiously, the hillside is festively adorned with white cherry blossoms.

Forchheim: the Bishop's Bastion

The narrow valleys of Franconian Switzerland were always less than suitable for the development of towns or cities. Therefore it is logical that the closest thing to a capital had to be situated in the foothills of the region. Forchheim is located at the mouth of the Wiesent, which provides water for almost all of Franconian Switzerland and empties into the Regnitz. The city is the gateway to the remote, rocky hillsides and enjoys the additional advantage that the Regnitz River happens to be one of the major north-south navigation routes in Germany. In the 7th century the Franks erected a base here that soon became an important royal court and later an imperial palace. Forchheim had a further important role to play when the bish-

opric in Bamberg was founded in 1007 and Forchheim became the second most powerful city after Bamberg. In the 16th century its power was expanded and the city served as the southernmost border fortification. The so-called imperial palace and the quaint half-timbered buildings on the Town Hall Square as well as some massive fortifying wall remnants are reminders of bygone days. The Anna Festival at the end of July offers the opportunity to literally get a taste of life in a tradition-conscious region. Beer flows aplenty throughout this celebration and hardly anyone really remembers the origin of such a festival: pious pilgrims ended their pilgrimage here on their way back from Anna Chapel in Weilersbach.

Strict Monks at Home in a Peaceful Setting

The Steigerwald Wood lies in the heart of Franconia and it is a peaceful place, something that is characteristic of the area between the Spessart Forest and the Fichtel Hills. Here, it is even more peaceful and

Above left: Forchheim's imperial palace served as a moated castle for the prince-bishops of Bamberg for hundreds of years.

Below left: The projecting structure across the Wiesent River increased the capacity of the Katherine Charitable Institution in the 17th century in Forchheim.

somewhat less spectacular. Gently rolling hills and meandering streams interspersed with copses, meadows and pastures dominate the scenery. The former Cistercian monastery, a cultural gem, lies tucked away in the remote Ebrach valley. The streambed in the wooded valley provided the perfect location for the recluse Cistercians. What began in the 12th century as a modest complex was turned into Baroque resplendence in the 18th century.

The facade of both the colossal church and adjacent St. Michael's Chapel are severe in design and reminiscent of the monastery's humble beginnings. The beautifully-dressed sandstone was symbolic of the glories of a heavenly Jerusalem and the prayers on the lips of these monks. "Ora et labora" - pray and work - was the maxim that ruled during construction of a second church in the 13th century. The large Baroque monastery complex is quite a dramatic contrast! It became a palace in which the abbots were more than willing to wear a princely crown as well as a miter. The irony of the story is that for hundreds of years the abbots fought to attain princely rank for their abbey but succeeded only once in being distinguished as such: in 1803 when the abbey was secularized.

Although the 19th century had no better use for the empty complex other than to convert the former monks' cells into prison cells for juvenile delinquents, Ebrach is still considered to be one of the most impressive abbey complexes in Germany.

Below right: Decorative half-timbered buildings surround the Town Square and St. Martin's in Forchheim.

Building Mania – a Fatal Illness

Lothar Franz von Schönborn, who commissioned the construction of the second most significant edifice in the Steigerwald Wood, Weißenstein Castle in Pommersfelden, was bent on having a showpiece from the very beginning. In 1711 Lothar Franz, elector of Mainz and prince-bishop of Bamberg rolled in one, had work begun on the Baroque castle, a wonderful memorial to his great love of art and to the Schönborn family. The necessary funds were the result of some contriving in which the elector cleverly arranged the election of Karl VI, a Hapsburg, as Emperor of the Holy Ro-

man Empire of the German Nation. In return, the emperor presented him with 100,000 guilders as a sign of his appreciation. This amount, however, was not sufficient to pay for an entire castle of this caliber with its sumptuous interiors and exquisite art collection; several of the Schönborn successors were required to continue this patronage of the arts. The debts were considerable, but what compulsive builder is really con-

Left: The ornate Baroque staircase in Ebrach Monastery stands in stark contrast to the otherwise humble premises of most Cistercian monks.

Above: The choir of the 13th century Ebrach monastery: a prayer in stone.

cerned about the price when suffering from such building fervor? The elector from Mainz was confident that his was a God-given role and that due to this role, craftsmen and artists found work. A tour of the castle designed by Johann Dientzenhofer is a fascinating trip back in time to the Baroque era and to the specific tastes of one single man, Lothar Franz. Rarely was a princely building commissioner in Germany so personally involved in a building's development, so filled with humor and so cultivated and knowledgeable as this Schönborn family member. It is indeed most fortunate that the current Schönborn family, who still uses the castle as a summer residence, has continued this long tradition of preserving the arts. Every summer young musicians are invited to perform within these magnificent walls.

For a few fleeting hours, the festive exuberance of the Grand Staircase and the Marble Hall in which the Collegium Musicum performs, returns the music lover to the former splendor of the days at court. The lavish rooms were originally designed as a backdrop for an ostentatious epoch in which grandeur was of utmost importance. A genuine understanding of life at court during the Baroque period is essential in or-

der to be able to suppress the astonished oohs and aahs of the tourist of the 21st century. Larger-than-life statues and oversized rooms and halls were as important as being able to withdraw to a private chamber to get away from the hustle and bustle of daily life. What was the purpose of having a Grand Staircase that was the size of an apartment building in our day and age? Nothing was merely purpose-built and space was never a concern. The Grand Staircase is best envisaged as a stage in which the most influential movers and shakers of the day were the actors. Every appearance on the Staircase was a performance and every performer

wanted to be entertained by his fellow actors in return. The construction of the Grand Staircase in Pommersfelden ensured the optimal setting: the ease with which a lady could glide up such a Staircase while her equals admired her from the upper galleries leaves nothing to the imagination except the extent of the spectacle itself. The Grand Staircase became a world theater and Rudolf Byss' ceiling frescos of

Above: Elector Lothar Franz von Schönborn had Weißenstein Castle built in Pommersfelden almost 300 years ago; his descendents still reside here.

231

the four known continents provided the appropriate audience and lent a good bit of confirmation to the splendor at hand. Other Grand Staircases such as the one in Versailles certainly set the standard, but the Grand Staircase's overall aesthetic beauty can definitely be attributed to the inspiration of Franz Lothar.

Franz Lothar von Schönborn also insisted on including all the exotic extras in his pleasure castle in order to ensure endless, entertaining leisurely hours. Weißenstein Castle contains the obligatory picture gallery as well as a Cabinet of Mirrors whose luxuriously mirrored walls lure the visitor into fairytale surroundings. In a similar way, the decorative shells and glittering stones alongside faux stalactite structures in the Grotto Room and the two adjoining rooms create a true fantasy world that nowadays takes some adjusting to. The Baroque mind, continually on the lookout for new earthly pleasures, grew ecstatic upon entering such a world.

Left: The full splendor of the Grand Staircase and its upper galleries proved ideal for the equally grand entrances of 17th century nobility.

Bamberg – A Picture-perfect City

If a country castle such as in Pommersfelden can emit so much grandeur, what do the neighboring cities in the Steigerwald Wood have to offer? The city of Bamberg is just as grand thanks to the Schönborns who made sure that this time-honored city also had a Baroque facelift in the 18th century. The Baroque facades are so perfect that a second or even third hard look is necessary in order to see just how old the city really is. The beginnings were in the year 1007 when Emperor Heinrich II was able to convince those gathered at an Imperial Diet in Frankfurt to found a new bishopric. The bishoprics of Würzburg and Eichstätt had been severely reduced to incorporate the plans of the Ottonian emperor. What wouldn't an emperor do for his empire? In fact, the founding of the bishopric gave the childless couple, Heinrich and Kunigunde, the opportunity to create something of their own. A construction boom began and after a few decades, the city built on supposedly seven hills was

quite a delightful sight. Bamberg was the quintessence of a medieval city whose religiosity was evident on every corner and in its churches. The medieval town center remains the heart of Bamberg even today even though the enthusiastic architects of the Baroque redid almost all of the churches, house fronts and the palace. Looking out from the tower of the Geyersworth Castle over to the edge of the Steigerwald Wood, the silhouette of the late Romanesque Cathedral, the crowning glory of the city, as well as Michelsberg Monastery and the Town Hall come into view.

The Cathedral Incorporates the Ideals of the Empire

The Cathedral of St. Peter and St. George has functioned as the Cathedral of the archbishop since 1817 when the almost unique position of the bishopric in Bamberg was honored by elevating it to this

Above: An overview of Bamberg's Old Town including the Cathedral, Michelsberg Monastery and the Town Hall seen from the tower of Geyersworth Castle.

235

new rank. It was the only bishopric in Germany that was under the direct influence of the pope in Rome. Moreover, this bishopric was founded by an emperor himself and therefore he had the political task of making it perfectly clear that he felt that he was just as much the head of Christianity as the bishop in Rome.

This involuntary dual role becomes most evident in the architecture of the two choirs. The west choir is dedicated to St. Peter and here is where the archbishop's seat is located as well as the tomb of the only pope to be buried in Germany. In contrast, the east choir represents worldly powers and is known as the imperial choir. In front of the steps leading up to

Above: The Bamberger Reiter or Bamberg Knight embodies the ideal knight in the Middle Ages.

Right: The Cathedral in Bamberg was built during the transitional period between the Romanesque and the Gothic.

236

the choir stands Tilman Riemenschneider's majestic tomb of the founders of the bishopric, Heinrich and Kunigunde, who were later canonized. St. George, the second patron saint of the Cathedral, represents the ideal of a Christian knight and stands in the east choir demonstrating his duty to protect both the church and Christianity. No other German Cathedral with a double choir incorporates the ideals of the empire in the high Middle Ages as decisively as in Bamberg.

Unadulterated Middle Ages – the Cathedral after its Purification

This Cathedral, dedicated in 1237, is still medieval in style. The reason no later generation "improved" on the structure was largely due to the Bavarian king, Ludwig I, and his enthusiasm for what he called a national memorial. Not only did he have his restorers remove everything that was not Romanesque or Gothic in style from the Cathedral, he even had the Ren-

aissance and Baroque effigies taken to the Michelsberg Monastery for safe-keeping. Many valuable works of art were never heard of again but what did survive has become even more significant. The all-important "Bamberger Reiter" or Bamberg Knight can be better appreciated now that he no longer has to compete with ornate Baroque statues. This knight, like the rest of the 13th sculpture in the Cathedral, would not have been possible without the French influence. Similarities to the sculpture work in Bamberg can be found in the French Cathedral in Reims. Even the knight had a predecessor; he is located in the so-called king's gallery in Reims and is not mounted but on foot. The art world has long debated exactly who this myste-

Left: Riemenschneider sculpted the tomb of the pious couple, Heinrich II and his wife, Kunigunde, who founded the bishopric in Bamberg. It has found an appropriate place n the nave of the Cathedral.

Below: Mature Romanesque architecture adorns the east crypt in the Cathedral.

rious knight could be. The assumptions vary from the ideal knight to an Ottonian emperor or a member of the Hohenstaufen dynasty to one of the Three Wise Men. Most likely it is the brother-in-law of Emperor Heinrich II, St. Stefan, the first Christian king of Hungary. The legend tells of him riding into the church to his own baptism in order not to appear as an ordinary petitioner. This would surely clarify the question as why we have a knight on horseback in a church.

Bamberg's Bishops Wore Both the Miter and the Crown

Bamberg's bishops were not only the spiritual leaders of their dioceses, after a few generations, they were also worldly princes in their bishoprics on the Upper Main and Regnitz rivers. The way of life of a prince-bishop in the high Middle Ages is easier to imagine in the Cathedral district of Bamberg than anywhere else in Germany. The Alte Hofhaltung or Old Royal Household with its steeply-gabled half-timbered structures demonstrates how closely linked administrative duties, representation and storage of the tithes were. Only the entry to the Cathedral Square is somewhat more representative with its ornate Renaissance chancellery. A decorative gate in the same style still acquaints the visitor with Heinrich and Kunigunde alongside other important figures on the Main and Regnitz rivers in order to symbolically outline the bishops' sphere of influence. This "Beautiful Gate" leads into a courtyard behind the asymmetrical building formerly resided in by prince-bishop Veit von Würtzburg. The late Gothic covered galleries that lead around the outer walls offer the perfect ambience for the Calderón Plays that are held here each summer. The Bamberg Historical Museum has also found a home within this ensemble.

Something More Modern – the New Residence

Baroque in the 18ᵗʰ century was not overly fond of medieval architecture or design; in fact, the Old Royal Household was to be torn down to make way for something more "modern". Prince-bishop Lothar Franz von Schönborn, a man known for his cultural good taste and building zeal, felt that the changes made in this structure over the course of time had left nothing more than architectural embarrassment. He commissioned the construction of the New Residence not far from the Old Royal Household. It was to be spacious and uniform in design and a palace that could compete with those in

Left: The Old Royal Household in Bamberg is one of the best preserved late medieval royal courts.

Below: The richly-decorated Renaissance façade of the council chambers built in the 1570s looks somewhat out of place in Bamberg.

other major cities such as Prague, Rome and Vienna. The task was given to the court architect, Johann Leonhard Dientzenhofer, who in 1703 completed the two wings that form the north and east sides of Cathedral Square. The west side is still flanked by the Old Royal Household, a true contrast to the super modern New Residence of the Schönborn epoch. The southwest corner of this Residence with its emerging stones still bears witness to the fact that an entire era was at the end of its tether financially. It wasn't solely the exterior that had to impress; the interior couldn't possibly end up being a disappointment either. Local Bamberg crafts-men as well as those brought in from elsewhere created a suite of apartments, a Cabinet of Mirrors and an Imperial Hall worthy of the prince-bishop of Bamberg. The Imperial Hall was kept in the traditional Baroque style that the prince-bishops were so fond of. This lavish hall is adorned with statues of 16 German emperors of the Holy Roman Empire and the ceiling fresco depicts the four known continents as well as the triumphal procession of the "Good Regiment" or government of the prince-bishops in the middle. On the first floor, the prince-bishop received his guests as the absolute ruler and upon his return from various travels, was able to report

that Bamberg was not merely culturally but also financially in its prime. The construction of the New Residence served the same function as holding the Olympics or a world exposition or building a major concert hall does nowadays. This was a public relations stunt to advertise Bamberg's important economic and political location. As magnificent as the apartments of the New Residence present themselves, one thing remains certain - great political decisions were rarely or very seldom made here. During the 18th century many of the prince-bishops of Bamberg were simultaneously the prince-bishops of Würzburg and personally preferred to spend their time

in the even more modern quarters of the Residence in Würzburg.

Napoleon, a Deposed Monarch, and a Government in Exile

When Bamberg finally became Bavarian in 1803, the New Residence became a second home for the Wittelsbach dynasty for more than the next hundred years. Nowadays, in addition to masterpieces of the late Baroque and the fine art collection of the Bavarian State Gallery, the New Residence displays the desk Napoleon personally wrote the "Declaration of War on Prussia" on in 1806. Moreover, Otto I, the first king of Greece, involuntarily spent the last four years of his life as a deposed king in this castle. After the Greeks had been freed of centuries of Turkish rule, this member of the Wittelsbach family became their king in 1833. In 1863, however, it became evident that the Bavarians and the Greeks had little in common other than their

Above: The four spires of St. Peter and St. Paul's Cathedral soar above the rooftops.

Left: Around 1700, Johann Dientzenhofer's New Residence next to the Cathedral was considered "a shock of modernity."

blue-white national colors. The Bavarian government unwillingly resided in Bamberg in 1919 when the Munich city council temporarily ran the government while Lenin toasted the new "Soviet Bavaria" on Moscow's Red Square during the May Day celebrations. Not only did Bamberg become the city in which a new type of citizen-oriented democratic constitution was ratified, it was also the place where the term "free state" of Bavaria was created.

Above: The Imperial Hall in the New Residence was where the prince-bishops received their guests.

Middle: The elegant audience chamber in the New Residence.

Right: A Chinese Chamber carved out of fruitwood was considered stylish during the Baroque epoch. Here porcelain from the Far East and counterfeit Delft porcelain could be grandly displayed.

Following pages: "Miniature Venice" is the name given to the fisherman's quarter on the bank of the Regnitz.

The Baroque Reconciled the Prince-bishop and the Townspeople

A significant municipal change occurred when the New Residence was built: Cathedral Square on the hill was opened to the

townspeople. Two street ramps were redesigned to provide a representational path up to the upper city where the canons and prince-bishop resided. It wasn't always the case that the clergy and the burghers were on friendly terms. More often than not, the two sides competed for political power with their gloves off. The fact that the canons within their secure walls also enjoyed legal immunity was another thorn in the eye of the burghers. Access to the New Residence on Cathedral Hill marked the beginning of the Baroque zeitgeist and these inequalities were literally and symbolically leveled out when the streets leading to Cathedral Hill were completed. Caught up in the spirit of the times, the burghers began to turn their homes into small palaces. Even the Town Hall that for generations had straddled the Regnitz and acted as a mediator between the town and the bishop, had to be adorned with frescoes. The citizens of Bamberg took the Baroque motto "seize the day" to heart and celebrated any and every festive occasion that came along. The occasion might have been a religious one such as the Corpus Christ Day procession, which was unparalleled in all of Germany, or a more secular festivity such as Sandkerwa held in the Sand quarter between

Above: Many pubs in Bamberg serve "Rauchbier" or smoked beer.

Below: A lively Fest takes place in the quaint Sandgasse every year.

Right: The Town Hall resembles a ship anchored in the Regnitz River. The bridge connects the bishop's quarter to the burghers' quarter.

Cathedral Hill and the river Regnitz. During these days of celebration, carpe diem and enjoying all of life's many pleasures were the only things that counted. Could there have been a more appropriate spot to celebrate these annual festivals than in Bamberg's intact Old Town? The city was never completely surrounded by a wall and perhaps that is the reason it never truly suffered heavy damages in an historical war. Even during World War II, in comparison to Würzburg or Nuremberg, Bamberg came away with only a few scratches. UNESCO made Bamberg's Old Town a World Heritage Site in 1993. Maintaining and preserving the city are tasks that are shared by the city's active citizens and the Bavarian state government. A newly-founded university in 1980 attracted many young people back to the narrow streets and lanes of the city. The individual university institutes and some of the dormitories have been incorporated into the lovingly-restored old buildings in the heart of Bamberg - a type of new spirit has come alive in the old structures.

New York and Franconian Rococo

The last Baroque building was yet to be built. Baroque architects never thought in terms of single structures; instead, these planners were set on going all the way and that included a retreat for the prince-bishop during the hot summer months, in other words, a summer residence. Seehof Castle in nearby Memmelsdorf became that summer retreat in 1687 and a 10-kilometer forest path was cut through the woods to connect it optically to the New Residence. The court architect in Würzburg, Antonio Petrini, considered the planned four-winged construction somewhat old-fashioned and thought it resembled the holiday version of the castle in Aschaffenburg.

Originally, the castle was to be called Marquard's Castle, named after Prince-bishop Marquard Sebastian Schenk von Stauffenberg who contracted the edifice. The locals called it Seehof or Lake Castle due to the fact that the castle was surrounded by so much water. The name stuck. When the castle was completed at the end of the 17th century, the prince-bishop's successors laid out a beautifully symmetrical 600 x 350 meter Baroque Garden that captured and enhanced the splendor of the castle. Prince-bishop Philipp Anton von Franckenstein commissioned the Bohemian sculptor, Ferdinand Tietz, to design the elegant and sometimes playful, polished sandstone statues throughout the garden. Walking through this lush green park past these jovial statues was like taking a walk through Classical mythology. Deities and heroes from the past such as Jupiter, Hercules and Minerva

had found a home in Seehof. Over 400 figures once adorned the park and only a few have survived. In the 19th century, the original castle itself was torn down. There might well have been a buyer or two after the bishopric was dissolved in 1803 but the castle was antiquated and no one was interested in maintaining the labor-intensive grounds. In 1842 the Prussian Hussar colonel, Friedrich von Zandt, purchased the entire package for 92,000 guilders, which he acquired through a marriage contract. His successors found little pleasure in the place and Seehof's downfall became imminent. The ponds were filled in and used, in part, as farmland. However, one

Left: High above the city, the former Michelsberg Benedictine Monastery still emits an air of august serenity.

Below: The Gothic choir of the Obere Pfarre Church justly represents the pride of the Bamberg patricians in the late Middle Ages.

pond too few was filled in: in 1951 the last Baron von Zandt drown in a castle pond whereupon his family had little choice but to sell all the interior furnishings. Entire rooms ended up in the Met in New York. It wasn't until the Free State of Bavaria bought the complex in the 70s that an interest in preserving and restoring the castle to its 18th century condition became an option. The most recent improvement was the completion of the unusual cascade fountain in 1995.

Left: The playful fountains in front of the sweeping Rococo staircase invite the visitor to linger and enjoy the more severe Baroque façade of Seehof Castle near Memmelsdorf.

Below: Ferdinand Tietz designed the ceruse statues as a study in Classical mythology in the Seehof Garden.

Following pages: Altenburg Fortress still manages to immerse the visitor into the Middle Ages.

Catholicism and the Reformation

Banz and Vierzehnheiligen, two lovely Baroque Catholic churches, adorn the wide valley of the Upper Main while the former duchy of Coburg is in Lutheran land.

A Poem for Franconia

"Well! the air is fresh and pure,
and idleness rusts the body.
The sky lets us delight
in the brightest sunshine.
Give me the staff and cloak
of the wandering scholar;
I want to make use of the summer
to travel to Franconia!"

The poet, Viktor von Scheffel, spent two months in Banz in 1859 and was deeply inspired by the countryside in and around the Upper Main River. Valentin Becker set his poem to music and turned it into the Franconian national anthem. Even though the text is not without its critics, it is at least true that the poet aptly described the splendid, wide Main valley. The main attractions in this region are two notable churches: the former monastery church of Banz and the pilgrimage church, Vierzehnheiligen (Fourteen Auxiliary Saints). The builders in the Baroque era were a most enthusiastic group of men and here as elsewhere, they chose an appropriate setting for their pious Catholic edifices. Like the twin columns of an open gate, both churches welcome the passer-by and emit a feeling of oneness with God and the world. It most certainly was not intentional, but when approaching from the German Protestant north, the two churches portray a type of triumphal gate through which one enters into Germany's Catholic south. The former Benedictine monastery of Banz crowns the steep hill north of the Main. The prominent team of Baroque

Previous pages: The wide Upper Main valley is in full view from the rocky outcrop of the Staffelberg.

Left: The impressive facade of Balthasar Neumann's pilgrimage church Vierzehnheiligen welcomes the pilgrim and art connoisseur alike.

Below: A bird's eye view of the former Benedictine monastery Banz reveals its true size.

architects, Dientzenhofer, Neumann and Küchel created an unforgettable facade to the glory of God. Since the middle of the 18th century, Balthasar Neumann's pilgrimage church, Vierzehnheiligen, has had its place opposite, across the valley atop a broad gentle hillside. Neumann's accomplishment here surpasses what was achieved at Banz. Pilgrims have been coming to this hillside spot for around 550 years to visit the miraculous place where once the Baby Jesus surrounded by fourteen auxiliary saints appeared before a shepherd. These saints are to be called on in times of need especially before a long journey. They include Erasmus and the wind, George and the dragon, Veit and the rooster, Katherine with the attributes of the wheel and sword and Barbara with the tower. A baldachin altar covers the holy spot in the sanctuary that wonderfully celebrates the belief in both God and miracles. Despite the fact that a Protestant architect had first been assigned the church-building task, Neumann succeeded in creating a unique world of light and dynamism that must be seen to be fully appreciated.

The "Franconian Crown" Protects Martin Luther

As so often is the case in Franconia, incompatibilities coexist side by side. It is a relatively short distance between the fragrance of an incense-burning pilgrimage church and a place of pilgrimage to the Reformation. Approaching from the state of Thuringia, the "Franconian Crown," the Veste Coburg with its silhouette of irregular gables and watchtowers, welcomes the traveler from across the Catholic Main valley. From Easter to the beginning of October in the year 1530, the Protestant Reformer, Martin Luther, stayed within the walls of these fortifications while his pa-

Left: The numerous towers protecting Veste Coburg have earned the fortifications the name of the "Franconian Crown."

261

tron, the Saxon elector, Johann the Constant, traveled to the Imperial Diet in Augsburg. Luther used his sojourn here to write theological doctrine as well as the Coburg Book of Psalms. Although the state rooms no longer contain much of the original furnishings, a visit to the rooms Luther stayed in and to the rich art collections of the former independent duchy of Saxe-Coburg is definitely worthwhile. The appearance of the Veste nowadays is mainly due to the patriotic efforts of the dukes of Coburg in the 19th and 20th centuries. Much of what had been destroyed was rebuilt and picturesquely restored in the hopes that it might become the home of the new German National Museum.

Wedding Suits for the Dukes

The German nation was often a guest in centrally-located Coburg. The duke sponsored the first German Gymnastics and Youth Festival in 1860 and two years later, the German Singers Association was established. Other nations as well were highly interested in the German province. In the 19th century, Coburg's most valuable export goods were monarchs! Leopold, the first king of Belgium and a man Napoleon called the most handsome in all of Europe, was one of these export triumphs. Later, Ferdinand, king of Portugal; Albert, husband of the English Queen

Victoria; and in 1887, a further Ferdinand, the czar of Bulgaria, all enjoyed positions of power abroad. Their advantage? They were not from a country that was eager to expand its borders and yet, they had the noble pedigree desired.

Coburg's charm has less to do with its connections to former monarchs; rather its charm lies in the unspoiled atmosphere and well-kept image of a city with a former palace. The Windsor-Gothic style of the exterior and, in part, the Italianate-Baroque interior of the palace in the middle of the city bear witness to the fact that the dukes of Coburg were among the first in Germany to have a so-called city residence among their subjects. In the 16th century a former Franciscan monastery was torn down to provide room for this palace, the Ehrenburg. Instead of a mendicant order and confessions, the duke displayed his metals and received guests.

Due to the unusual fact that all of the craftsmen were actually paid for their skills,

Above: The princely quarters in the Veste Coburg now house art treasures from the counts of Coburg.

Left: The incongruous church towers of St. Moriz's in the foreground; the Coburg Fortifications in the background.

Following pages: The Berlin architect, Karl Friedrich Schinkel, gave Ehrenburg Castle in the heart of Coburg its neo-Gothic facade in the 19th century.

263

which was something to be proud of, the emperor himself decided that the castle would be called Ehrenburg, which roughly translates into Palace of Honor. An overabundance of the Baroque style rich in stuccowork dominates in the White Hall and the Hall of Giants. The latter is named after the 28 large caryatids that jet out of the walls and provide support for the huge ceiling.

Across the street, plays and concerts are performed much in the same way as in the time of the dukes. Coburg remains a small "state" capital with pleasant, narrow winding streets. Moreover, the citizens here pride themselves on being more Bavarian than anyone else in the Free State of Bavaria. After all, the inhabitants of the Coburg Land region were the only ones that ever decided of their own accord that they wanted to

become Bavarian. During a voting initiative in 1920, they demonstratively voted down a petition to become a part of the newly-founded state of Thuringia.

Ever since, the region has been under the administrative auspices of Upper Franconia. However, spend a few minutes at the Market Square and the lively arguments among the locals in Franconian dialect about the varying qualities of bratwurst are proof enough that this group of people really is at home in Bavaria. South American dialects and music among the dancers in the streets during the Samba Summer Carnival don't seem to bother a soul.

Above: For over 300 years now, 28 Baroque atlases have played their dual role of lending support and grandeur to Ehrenburg Castle.

Historic Houses against the Backdrop of Densely-forested Hills

The northeastern part of Franconia

is more rugged in appearance;

the Franconian Forest and the

Fichtel Hills are austere, wooded

regions. The Markgrafenland

region surrounding Bayreuth and

Kulmbach offers cultural treasures.

The East-West Border Disappears

Before German reunification, the seemingly never-ending border between East and West Germany ran along the edge of the densely wooded Franconian Forest. For over forty years the Franconian Forest, actually in the heart of a united Germany, forced this economically weak region into remoteness. In 1989 when the border disappeared, the geological unity of the Franconian Forest and the Thuringian Wood finally became politically reunited as well. The expected economic upswing on both

Previous pages: The water rushes through the narrow Steinach Gorge.

Above: Dammed-up water forces the rafts downstream.

Below: A charcoal burner at work: this dying trade was once a common sight in the Franconian Forest.

Following pages: The Franconian Forest remains sparsely settled. A limited amount of cultivated land can be found on its outskirts.

sides of the border has yet to occur. There is no noticeable border within the forest but the dialects differ and the buildings vary in structure. Both the Franconian and Thuringian dialect can be heard. Yet as long as the streams flow into the Main River, the Franconian Forest will remain Franconian at heart.

Mitwitz, a moated castle, stands on the border between the Coburg Land region and the Franconian Forest, on the edge of the deep dark woods. Although it isn't as well-known as the castle of Mespelbrunn in the Spessart Forest, it is worth the detour. The castle's noble reflection in the moat says it all. Built after the Peasants' War, the Renaissance castle with its multiple towers, inner courtyard and draw bridges, has an air of self-confidence about it that makes it clear that the Rosenau and Würtzburg families were far from provincial. Although a member of the Würtzburg family became prince-bishop in Bamberg and several other family members became canons in Würzburg, the two had nothing in common outside the similarity in their names.

Rosenberg – a Mighty Fortress

As sparsely-populated as the Franconian Forest is, it is clear that it cannot compete culturally with the other more heavily-endowed parts of Franconia. Yet there are a number of jewels in this region such

as the thousand-year old town of Kronach located on the confluence of the Haßlach, the Kronach and the Rodach. The town was always predestined to become a hub of activity since from its beginning, it was the point of intersection of the many valleys and hills in the region. If a town is of importance, it must be properly fortified and that is precisely what the prince-bishops in Bamberg had in mind. This was their fortress and their "key to the hills" from the late Middle Ages to the end of the Holy Roman Empire of the German Nation in 1803. Rosenberg Fortress takes on a somewhat squatty but mighty appearance on the hill above Kronach and that was the secret to its success: it offered the enemy practically no room to maneuver or attack. This pentagon of spiritual power, this, the mightiest fortress in the entire bishopric of Bamberg, was never forced to admit enemy troops voluntarily, but the fortifications had to continually be fitted out with the latest in military technology. When Bishop Otto had living quarters including a tower built of stone in 1130, he was actually having the foundation stone of the present fortress laid. Not until the early 18th century, however, were the fortifications as we see

them today. The small upper town of Kronach, which seems more like a large fortified courtyard in front of the fortress, has the distinction of being the loveliest Old Town in the Franconian Forest region. Surrounded by a protective wall, the upper town successfully withstood innumerable sieges, but at the same time, the fact that it was fortified hindered its economic development. The past decade has brought some prosperity to the town. A Bavarian Garden Show attracted many tourists and

Above: Rosenberg Fortress, protected by its mighty bastion, sits on the hill above Kronach. It is one of the few fortifications in Germany that was never taken by enemy forces.

Left: The Bamberg Gate and the medieval wall surrounding the upper town in Kronach survived three military attacks from the Swedish during the Thirty Years' War.

the opening of a branch of the Bavarian State Galleries in the Rosenberg Fortress has made the region more attractive to the culturally-inclined. Furthermore, Kronach is the birthplace of one of Germany's greatest painters, Lucas Cranach.

A Growing Export Item: Wood

Kronach's streams disappear quickly into the woods. Once there were fir trees; nowadays pine trees or deciduous trees grow here. The people in this region made good use of the forested areas since growing crops was not a viable option. Thus the forest became a source of revenue: surplus stone and wood. The logs were shipped as far as the Netherlands where they were used as building materials for everything from ships and houses to furniture and beer kegs. Most of the fir or pine trees that

are more or less forced to roll up your sleeves to make ends meet. The Franconian Forest region along with its neighbor, the Vogtland region, as well as the Fichtel Hills have turned this part of the country into one of the cradles of Franconian industry. The price to be paid was no small one and it is apparent in many of the towns. Almost every city and many of the villages burned down at least once in the 19th century leaving the northeasterly part of Franconia devoid of historical Old Towns.

originated in the dark valleys of the Franconian Forest saw more of the world than the workers who sent these tree trunks on their way. If not beforehand, the construction of the various locks in the Main River finally put an end to log transport on rafts. There were, of course, clever log drivers who could maneuver their rafts through any narrow lock. Nowadays rafting is nothing more than a leisure time sport. Wood processing didn't necessarily need to be carried out elsewhere. Like the charcoal burners who knew how to turn their wood into coal, there were enough skilled furniture-builders and toy-makers in the region as well. Stone, especially slate, was the region's second export product. Slate roofs and facades are popular throughout Franconia, and, slates were also used to write on - every now and then a pupil might have felt completely vexed while staring at an empty slate.

Necessity is the mother of invention as the saying goes and if you don't happen to live in the land of milk and honey, you

Above: A 19th century renovation that included larger windows turned Lauenstein Fortress into a comfortable home.

Right: Lauenstein Fortress, situated near the Thuringian border, stands proudly in the Loquitz valley.

This fact makes a visit to Lauenstein Fortress not far from the Thuringian border a very pleasant surprise. Lauenstein Fortress has managed to survive the ravages of time. It dates back to the 13th century when it was known as Löwenstein Fortress and started ruling over the narrow Loquitz valley. The powerful counts of Orlamünde, the same counts who eventually became the margraves of Brandenburg-Bayreuth, maintained and occupied the fortress complex whenever the necessity arose. Nowadays, the Bavarian government maintains this fairytale castle which is a combination of Gothic, Renaissance and naturally, a bit of 19th century Romantic architecture.

The Town of Hof in the Heart of the Vogtland Region

The 19th century marks the real beginning of the town of Hof. It is actually outside the Franconian Forest but it is the ideal geographical center of the eastern foot-

hills. To be even more precise, Hof is the center of the Bavarian Vogtland region and this region crosses the border into the eastern states of Thuringia and Saxony, and extends as far as Bohemia. It is transit country and a part of the world that depends on transit trade. For this very reason, the Vogtland region suffered more by being cut off during the Cold War than any other region either side of the border. Like many other towns in the region, Hof is a typical 19th century town. In 1823 a huge fire burned 90% of all the buildings in the commercial town. Rebuilding the town in the Biedermeier era resulted in a look of subdued uniformity that was typical of the time. Moreover, it was also in the 19th century that Hof's ubiquitous bratwurst venders, known as "Wärschtlamoo" began recommending an excursion to Theresienstein, a 70-hectare civic park not far from the town. The town's citizens had the land for the park set aside in 1817 to ensure a recreational area with many leisure time attractions.

Whoever has a penchant for long woodsy walks combined with the atmosphere of

Above: Hof's stately Town Hall, built after a fire in 1832, remains an arresting symbol of will.

Right: In the 19th century, the residents of Hof created Theresienstein Park for their own leisure time enjoyment.

a spa resort should pay a visit to the neighboring towns of Berneck and Bad Steben. The tiny spa town of Steben, situated in the Franconian Forest near the Thuringian border and the Saale valley, offers unique carbonic acid baths and all-natural moor baths. It was exactly 175 years ago that the Kingdom of Bavaria acquired this spa where people had been taking the waters since the 15th century. The kingdom paid 600 guilders for the hamlet and created an extremely elegant spa resort in the Biedermeier style. Leo von Klenze, the court architect of Ludwig I's, was sent to this new remote corner of Bavarian to erect a bathhouse befitting of royalty. The improved infrastructure benefited the weak economy in the Franconian Forest. The

Above: A typical scene and typical hues in the Franconian Forest.

Middle: Nineteenth century luxury in the spa town of Berneck which specializes in mineral and moor baths.

Right: The charming Pump Room in the spa park in Bad Steben.

famous German natural scientist, Alexander von Humboldt, had failed at such an attempt just three decades earlier. Commissioned between 1793 and 1795 by the Prussian government in Berlin, Humboldt did reinvigorate the mining of iron ore for a short period and even started a mining school in the Franconian Forest and the

Fichtel Hills. Visitors can still follow in Humboldt's footsteps through the historical tunnel in neighboring town of Lichtenberg. In the long run, however, mining was not economically viable and capitalizing on the mineral waters in Steben seemed to be an easier method of utilizing the mineral resources of the region. If you aren't into the medicinal side of spa resorts, you are welcome to try out your luck in the new casino there.

Bastions and Beer in Kulmbach

The margraves of Brandenburg-Bayreuth were the strongest political power in the Upper Main region after the prince-bishops in Bamberg. They left their distinct mark throughout the entire eastern part of Upper Franconia. Their first residence was Kulmbach or Plassenburg Fortress,

situated high above the beer metropolis on the White Main River. In 1397 the fortress, having been expanded in size, became the home of the Hollenzollern dynasty, the burgraves in Nuremberg. The settlement at the foot of the hill began to grow as well and the heart of the town formed around the fortified church of St. Peter's. As the significance of the fortress grew, the town also expanded in the direction of the White Main. Kulma, from the Slavic for hill stream, was the name of the settlement first documented in the 11th century. The name survives today in its corrupted version "Kohlenbach," the name of the stream that flows through the town. The town revolved in and around the lords in Plassenburg Fortress but from early on, textile manufacturing and beer brewing brought prosperity to the inhabitants. According to local tradition, the reason that Kulmbach beer is so

well-known outside the borders of Franconia is due to the wagon-drivers who always carried a keg of beer with them in case they got thirsty. And naturally, these wagon-drivers often shared their beer with others who after a large swig wanted more of the stuff. Thus, especially after the trade routes were improved in the 19th century, there was a huge increase in the export of Kulmbach beer. Statistically seen: 166 hectoliters were exported in 1831 while the amount climbed to 663,023 hectoliters in 1897. Nowadays four large breweries do their best to prevent anyone from getting a parched throat. The Bavarian Brewery Museum provides information on the history of brewing in the town.

Pure Renaissance and Loose Women

Another supra-regional museum in Kulmbach is in Plassenburg Fortress, the town's landmark and home of the German Tin Figure Museum since 1932. More than

300,000 tin figures effectively bring world history to life. Where else can the museum-goer watch poachers hunting mammoths in the Ice Age, see Hagen drop the treasure of the Nibelungen into the Rhine or view Bavarian King Ludwig II on an evening sleigh ride? The tin figures and paper maché sets are indeed entertaining but the fortifications deserve a closer look as well. Although the interior is no longer furnished in the style of the sumptuous celebrations of a noble court, the fortress is, nevertheless, one of the best examples of a fortified complex that simultaneously served as a residential castle. Visitors continue to be astounded by the great contrast between the intact bastions that

Above: Foreboding Plassenburg Fortress dominates the hilltop above Kulmbach, which is famous for its beer breweries.

Right: Kulmbach's Baroque Town Hall and fountain seem more inviting than the fortress; the Market Square is in the background.

threatened the approaching enemy and the extravagant charm of the Beautiful Courtyard. Three sides of the central courtyard are decorated with a double arcade of highly-ornate relief design that gives the appearance of being an outdoor festive hall. Casper Vischer created this superb work of art in the 1560s and it is the epitome of what the German Renaissance has to offer. A compliment must be paid to margrave Georg Friedrich von Ansbach who commissioned Vischer and gave him free rein and a very generous annual salary. The portraits of the individual members of court decorate the parapets of the arcades. The appealing courtyard welcomed a variety of guests. In 1847 during a visit to Plassenburg Fortress, the travel writer, Ludwig Braunfels, commented: "the castle ... has been turned into a prison for thieves and loose women." Kulmbach and its fortress became Bavarian in

1810 and the new rulers weren't able to come up with a better use for the fortifications than to turn them into a military hospital, a state-run weaving mill operated by forced laborers, a prison and finally a prisoner-of-war camp. It wasn't until 1928 that the artistic and cultural value of Plassenburg again became evident.

Thurnau – a Type of Capital as Well

Kulmbach paves the way into the land of the margraves for the traveler heading up the Main. Every now and again, various other family lines were able to maintain their freedom and independence in this region. It was Franconia more than any other region that offered pockets of independence for lesser nobility and the lesser aristocracy. This phenomenon is well-illustrated in Thurnau Castle and the village

and a Protestant parish church. The Lower Castle is medieval and the ladies' bower complete with fireplace within is the oldest part. Actually, the word fortress would be more suitable for this part of the complex. An unusual feature is the arcaded passage across the main street between the Lower Castle and the parish church. This was a very convenient way for the lords to enter the church. The majority of the

of the same name, which are situated south of Kulmbach where the rock from the Jurassic Period becomes lighter in color. Here is where the Förtsch von Thurnau family was able to defend itself successfully against the margraves of Kulmbach, who were far superior in strength. The family controlled a total of ten villages and three fortresses, of which Thurnau was considered the "capital." A biological factor succeeded where the margraves failed: in 1564, the male line of the family died out and the females who were left to inherit the family holdings were soon married off to career-oriented sons of other noblemen. The Künßberg and the Giech families shared the land holdings until 1731 when the Giech family bought out the Künßberg family and ruled over these holdings alone. Thurnau's checkered history comes alive in the exceedingly charming complex consisting of an Upper Castle, Lower Castle

Above: The Beautiful Courtyard of Plassenburg Fortress is renowned for its detailed stone décor. A closer glimpse reveals some members of the royal court.

Right: Some of Germany's finest Renaissance arcades flank the Beautiful Courtyard.

buildings, however, were completed in the 16th and 17th centuries and during this period, the original upper fortress or Upper Castle was turned into a castle in the true sense of the word including a fountain in the courtyard. The Giech family line resided in the complex in the 19th century preserving its historical past. Later owners were financially unable to maintain the castle. Nowadays the University of Bayreuth uses the complex in part as a research institute for musicals.

The Search for the Odyssey in Upper Franconia

"Ma foi, Monseigneur, c'est san pareil!" were the words of the court manager of

the margrave couple the first time they visited the rock garden near the old Zwernitz Fortress. Those words stuck and from then on, both the village and the spectacular new park had a name: Sanpareil - without equal. What was so marvelous about this garden? Moreover, what kind of sensation could be expected in this remote part of the world? It was the scenery that with a bit of help became the setting for a fantastic story. The story and the location were meant for each other and Countess Wilhelmine von Bayreuth was the ideal director. It was in the spring of 1744 that the countess discovered the beech grove interspersed with unusual rock formations. Her imagination immediately got the best of her and a short time later she found some caves and named them Calypso's Grotto, Vulcan's Grotto and Cupid's Grotto. The French writer Fénelon, who functioned as the archbishop on the side, supplied the script for her in his book "The Adventures of Telemachus," where he described the daring deeds of Telemachus during his search for his father, Odysseus. Fénelon did more than just tell a simple story, he filled the book with instructive material as well as social criticism and thus fell into disfavor with his king. Countess Wilhelmine was not only impressed by the scenic beauty surrounding her, she also most certainly shared the rather rebellious ideas of the French author. With the assistance of her court architect, Saint Pierre, between 1745 and 1748, Wilhelmine created the most unique garden of the epoch. It was neither French nor English in design; instead, it was a blend of original architectural creations in a landscaped setting. The small Oriental castle, for instance, encircles a live tree. A theater ruin is just as unusual: the theater-goer feels weighed down by its massive rock walls and the stage doubles as a garden facade. The garden emits an air of melancholy in many spots and not solely because some of the architec-

Left: A covered passage conveniently joins Thurnau's castle to its church.

287

ture has not survived. The countess' presence, her oversensitive soul, still permeates the grottos and rock formations. There actually once was a small temple perched atop a rocky precipice that was dedicated to "Le Contentement perdu." Here, Wilhelmine shed many a tear for her unfaithful husband who was in love with her closest friend. A true garden of sensitivity and thus sans pareil.

A Street Market Becomes a City with a Palace

In comparison to Sanpareil, Bayreuth is a genuine capital and in fact, it is the capital of Upper Franconia with a population of approximately 70,000. Bayreuth's charm is due to the margraves' penchant for not staying in one place over a longer period of time. Exactly 400 years ago, upon being fed up with his living quarters in the outdated Plassenburg Fortress above Kulmbach, margrave Christian moved to the broad valley of the Red Main. The farm settlement of "Baierrute"

Above: The perfect natural frame for Zwernitz Fortress from the Sanspareil Gardens.

Rigth: The theater as a ruin in the Sanspareil Gardens.

288

or farmer's switch began to flourish almost immediately and attracted other lesser nobility and civil servants. However, the sumptuous castle on the hill was actually rather modest due to a lack of funds. By the time Wilhelmine, sister of Friedrich II of Prussia, married margrave Friedrich, her description of what she found waiting for her was hardly euphoric. She described the Great Hall in the Old Castle as follows: "I walked into a large room whose Old Franconian ceiling was the main decoration; the upper wall frieze was presumably ... lovely at one time but when I saw it, it was so old and faded that I would have needed a microscope to decipher the former pattern. The figures were life-size and the faces so full of holes and smeared that they resembled ghosts." It is easy to see what a great challenge awaited this creative lady. She was indeed successful in turning this dingy provincial castle into an elegant Rococo castle of muses. Fortunately, the Old Castle previously described went up in flames in 1753 and the couple was forced to rebuild elsewhere. The New Castle wasn't exactly an architectural masterpiece but the sophistication and soft colors of the elegant interior makes it comparable to the best of German Rococo. Floral garlands of delicate buds and cordons of blossoms, trellises, mirrors and palm trees create an unusual, unique personal touch. This cas-

tle is proof enough that good taste can go a long way in supplementing a shortage of funds.

A Great Theater: the Margrave's Opera House

Before having the New Castle built, Wilhelmine and her husband had been able to afford to have an Opera House built - an absolute must for an aristocratic family especially since Wilhelmine was such an accomplished poet, composer and musician. Joseph Saint-Pierre was responsible for the facade and the Bolognese theater specialist, Giuseppe Galli Bibiena, was the master craftsman of the interior, a "perpetual theater" as he called it. There is barely a trace of the light and

airy Rococo that Wilhelmine cherished so dearly in the Opera House that was completed in 1748. The interior is of powerful grandiose design; the greens and golds add to the theatricality and lofty pompousness. The stage itself takes up half of the interior and a walk through it makes it at once clear that this theater was the real festive Great Hall of the entire line of margraves. There are only a

handful of such marvelous Baroque theaters left in Germany; Bayreuth can count itself fortunate to have such an ambiance in which to perform Monteverdi or Handel.

Where Wagner Had his Say

Was it this Opera House that convinced Richard Wagner to settle down in Bayreuth? Not in the least! The technical limitations of the theater were too great a hindrance for his performances, the stage too small and the decor far too domineering. Whoever has been fortunate enough to get a ticket to a Wagner opera performed at the Festspielhaus on the "Green Hill" understands why the Opera House wasn't suited for the forceful operatic masterpieces of a genius like Wagner. Lohengrin, Parsifal, Siegfried and all the oth-

Left: Margrave Christian Ernst as a majestic equestrian in front of the New Castle in Bayreuth.

Above: Fruitwood paneling in the Palm Room in the New Castle is an original creation of the Rococo era in Bayreuth.

291

ers need a room that is filled by their presence alone. No extra paraphernalia or balderdash, no fancy entrance for the nouveau riche opera-goers and definitely no affectations to distract from the total immersion into the world of Wagner. That is basically the reason that the Festspielhaus or Festival Hall largely resembles a barren barn or even an airplane hangar. Why then did Wagner choose Bayreuth? Mainly because Wagner wanted a venue in central Germany and in the land of his financial savior, Ludwig II. Wagner wanted to perform neither in a resort town where people might come for reasons other than Wagnerian music nor a spa town since he felt spa tourists were disinterested, uneducated or simply frail. Bayreuth became the town that best suited Wagner's fancies.

Beer Lures Poets

The poet Jean Paul was of a different breed. He, it is said, came for the beer. "A vat of beer makes me happier than the news of a newborn baby..." he once said of himself. There is most probably some truth behind these words since Jean Paul is also quoted as having said "If something doesn't go to my head, it shouldn't head for my bladder either." Be that as it may, he brought fame to Bayreuth by putting the city on the literary map and puzzled quite a few readers. The highly-imaginative poet's wandering thoughts and manifold footnotes are not easy to digest.

Wilhelmine, Richard Wagner and Jean Paul, Bayreuth's triumvirate, form the historical "loci genius" but the present city of Bayreuth is noteworthy as well. Bayreuth is prospering. That is made evi-

Below: An unusual bridge between the spires of the City Church in Bayreuth saved the tower warders many an unnecessary ascent.

Right: A breathtaking example of a Baroque Protestant church in the Bayreuth region. In St.George's, the pulpit is above the altar and the organ is under the roof.

dent by the industrial estates and suburbs mushrooming up on the outskirts of the Old Town. A new university should help keep the town young.

The Hermitage: Glorious Asceticism

There seems to be no end to the influence of the margraves. Leaving Bayreuth in the direction of the Fichtel Hills, the Hermitage soon comes into view. The name implies the home of a man, who lives a secluded life. Bayreuth's hermitage evokes a very different impression - here is an 18th century elegant summer retreat in an artificially landscaped setting. It all began in the 17th century as a zoological park. In the 18th century margrave Georg Wilhelm decided to build a small hermitage castle like other aristocrats were having built. If Louis XIV could

Left: The theater of the margrave's Opera House in Bayreuth is a performance in itself.

Below: Wagnerian pilgrims gather here at the Festive Hall on the Green Hill in Bayreuth.

have one, why shouldn't a margrave. The result is a curious mixture of castigated barrenness intermingled with a delightful ambiance. Wilhelmine was involved here too. An elegant crescent structure on either side of a Sun Temple forms the backdrop for a large pond containing 58 fountains adorned with stones, shells and mythical figures. The landscaped park with its grotto, cave and idyllic ruins also contains the gravestone of Wilhelmine's best friend, her dog Folichon.

The densely-forested Fichtel Hills can be seen off to the east of Bayreuth. The hills rise to over 1,000 meters making them the highest in Franconia. The White Main river valley between Ochsenkopf and Schneeberg forms a natural path into these hills. Water from the Erlenbach Stream flows into the White Main from a narrow side valley where the spa town of Berneck lies safe and sound. Alexander von Humboldt and Richard Wagner came here to drink the waters and relax before the town officially became a spa. The serene Market Square is enclosed by half-timbered buildings and the ruins of a medieval stronghold rise behind the

square resulting in a picture-perfect Old Franconian ensemble. The arcaded walkways are a type of unpretentious calling card for the famous Bohemian springs.

Granite, Weatherworn Formations and Tree after Tree

The Fichtel Hills are more or less horseshoe in shape opening up to the east. Berneck is located on the western edge of the horseshoe but the hills already seem overpowering with their endless rows of coniferous trees interspersed with the occasional cultivated clearing. Wunsiedel in the center of the horseshoe marks the end of the wooded area. Stone though, is just as prevalent here as trees. Hard, fine-grained granite is the basis of these hills. Although this granite is used for gravestones and kitchen counters far outside the region, the granite can best be appreciated in its natural setting as it jets out unexpectedly from a sea of fir trees and takes on bizarre shapes and formations. It isn't a simple matter getting to the lookout points in the Fichtel Hills; the rock climber is probably best-equipped to do so. The most spectacular of these weatherworn formations have

an extremely resilient outer surface. In the case of one particular granite formation, the outer surface was much harder than the outer surfaces elsewhere and therefore over time, the softer outer surfaces weathered away leaving this particular granite formation standing isolated and alone. This remaining formation is of great interest to geologists studying the different layers of stone. In this case Mother Nature was very accommodating

Above and left: The New Castle and fountains of the Hermitage located just outside Bayreuth make it a favorite meeting place.

297

to mankind but nature as a whole is far more interesting when there is little rhyme or reason behind a strikingly bizarre rock formation such as the popular Luisenburg labyrinth. Even Johann Wolfgang Goethe returned day after day to roam through this rocky maze that is unique in Germany. The Luisenburg doubles as an open air theater during the summer months and derived its name from the Prussian queen, Luise.

Water Flows in all Directions

The highest peak in the Fichtel Hills, the Schneeberg or Snow Mountain, is exactly 1046.23 meters high and confirms its name winter after winter. Bishofsgrün, an old farming settlement, is not far away and it offers lodging for hikers in the summer and regional skiers in the winter. Due to global warming, the winters aren't as cold as they once were but the air is crisp and clear and the scenery invigorating. Across the valley from the Schneeberg is the prominent Ochsenkopf or Ox's Head, the locals' so-called "home hill." It doesn't derive its name from the animal but from the Celtic word for source or spring. The saddle between the hills wasn't formed by some meadow or forest stream although it looks as if it could have been. The saddle was formed by the White Main River, one of the two source streams of the Main River which is Franconia's main navigational route. The Fichtel Hills are full of springs and streams and water flows abundantly in literally every possible direction. It supplies the Saale River to the north, the Eger to the east near Bohemia and the Naab flows south into the Danube. The Main River flows and meanders westwards for 524 kilometers before it empties into the Rhine making it the longest westward-flowing river in Germany. The rivers tell the real story: the Fichtel Hills are in the center of Europe!

Wunsiedel, "White Gold," and Pleasant Memories at the End of the Excursion

Franconia continues across the hills into the valley of the Eger River. Wunsiedel is the next traditional stopover. Once a town whose walls were "marble-faced," nowadays Wunsiedel presents itself as a

friendly, pleasant mid-19th century town. After the devastating fire in 1834, the town was modestly rebuilt in a simple Classical style with the streets laid out in a logical manner. As in many other towns that had to be rebuilt in the 19th century, a certain amount of direction and influence from the government in Munich was inevitable. The works of architects like Klenze and Gärtner in the Bavarian capital were the prototypes. The largest undertaking was the reconstruction of the Town Hall which was designed by the local architect, Johann Andreas Ritter, in the late Classical style. The second most important building to be re-erected, the Gewerbeschule or Vo-

Left: Fichtel Lake, Franconia's highest lake, is slowly filling in.

Above: A bright, snowy winter day in the Fichtel Hills.

Middle: Wooden planks "cap" the homes in this region.

299

regional workforce. Selb, the center of "white gold," is located in the far eastern corner of Upper Franconia. Hutschenreuther, Heinrich and Rosenthal are the town's renowned porcelain manufacturers who have made a name for themselves throughout the four corners of the globe. Eighty percent of Germany's porcelain is manufactured in the Fichtel Hills. Moreover, this region has the highest concentration of porcelain manufacturing in the world. Porcelain manufacturers are having their problems nonetheless. Bohemian porcelain, manufactured at around half the price, is be-

cational School, was constructed according to the plans of none other than Friedrich von Gärtner. At least the Baroque Parish Church survived the fire in 1834 but burned down in 1903. It took three years to be reconstructed in the same fashion using many of the salvaged building materials. The numerous fountains throughout the town are still maintained and the appropriate setting for the annual Fountain Festival held each summer. The festival recalls the extremely long dry period that the town suffered until a "miracle" caused the fountains to flow again.

Fires were common in those days in the forested hills where trade and industry were at home. The situation here was similar to the one in the Franconian Forest; the locals were forced to be resourceful and come up with a means of making a decent living. Ironworks, mines, stone quarries and panning for gold did and in part, still do provide jobs for the

Above: This spring in the Fichtel Hills starts out as a thin stream which eventually feeds into the White Main River.

Right: Primordial stone formations in the Fichtel Hills offer wide views of the pristine countryside.

Following pages: Luisenburg Labyrinth near Wunsiedel rates as Germany's largest sea of rocks.

ing manufactured practically next door. The reopened borders to the east signify a variety of opportunities and benefits, but at the same time, more competitive prices. Here along the immediate eastern border, the opportunities will be taken advantage of while the disadvantages are being confronted. If the Franconians have learned one thing throughout their long history in Germany and in the middle of Europe, they have learned that composure and a smile are as important as buckling down to hard work. The riflemen in Wunsiedel appropriately proved this point during the War of Liberation from 1812-13. Their targets had the following slogan:

The world is a dungeon
That no one finds pleasure in.
Our joy can turn the world
Into a paradise.

No Clear Borders

The eastern portion of Upper Franconia doesn't have any sharp contours or real borders. Crossing over into the Saxony or the Thuringian parts of the Vogtland region go unnoticed. A visit to the churches in the Saxony or Thuringian parts of the region, however, reveals a sharp distinction, namely one of religious belief. While the Protestant faith remained rather restrained in its church decor in the land of the former margraves, the churches in the Oberpfalz region, especially after the Counter-Reformation, virtually became architectural guides for the opulence and the pleasures of life in the Baroque era. The church in Waldsassen is a good example. Upon entering the sanctuary, the traveler has the feeling that the craftsmen would have considered it a deadly sin to leave even a mere centimeter undecorated. Every square centimeter has been adorned with sumptuous stuccowork, frescoes and angels. The view makes one feel pious.

The Pilgrimage Church of Kappel is located near the Upper Franconian border. Georg Dientzenhofer, a well-known architect of the period, was commissioned to incorporate the mystery of the Holy Trinity into the church's architecture. Dientzenhofer gladly took up the challenge and successfully created one of the most original Baroque churches in all of Germany. Three half circles extend from the sides of a triangle that forms the center of the church. The three altars in each of these niches symbolize the Father, Son and Holy Ghost as do the three onion towers adorned by three lanterns on the outside. From a certain distance, the church appears like an orthodox mirage on the horizon. The better the church comes into view, the clearer the concept of the Holy Trinity becomes. It is rare that an architect is in the position to transform a symbolic floor plan into such architectural perfection.

As previously mentioned, the eastern part of Upper Franconia reveals a character entirely its own. Somewhat matter-of-fact, practical and Protestant in nature. Nothing makes this fact as clear as a visit to the pilgrimage church in Kappel. A short detour into the "Old Bavarian" part of the world is well worth the effort since the contrast becomes immediately self-evident. This is perhaps a fitting place to end our journey.

Above: Kappel Pilgrimage Church near Waldsassen – the Holy Trinity in stone.